Introducing Gradle

Balaji Varanasi
Sudha Belida

Apress®

Introducing Gradle

ISBN-13 (pbk): 978-1-4842-1032-1

ISBN-13 (electronic): 978-1-4842-1031-4

Managing Director: Welmoed Spahr
Lead Editor: Steve Anglin
Technical Reviewer: Manuel Jordan Elera
Editorial Board: Steve Anglin, Mark Beckner, Louise Corrigan, Jonathan Gennick,
    Robert Hutchinson, Michelle Lowman, James Markham, Susan McDermott,
    Matthew Moodie, Jeffrey Pepper, Douglas Pundick, Ben Renow-Clarke, Gwenan Spearing
Coordinating Editor: Mark Powers
Copy Editor: Kezia Endsley
Compositor: SPi Global
Indexer: SPi Global
Artist: SPi Global

Contents at a Glance

Contents

About the Authors

Balaji Varanasi is a software development manager, author, speaker, and technology entrepreneur. He has over 14 years of experience architecting and developing high-performance, scalable Java and .NET mobile applications. During this period, he has worked in the areas of security, web accessibility, search, and enterprise portals. He has a master's degree in computer science from Utah State University and serves as adjunct faculty at the University of Phoenix, teaching programming and information system courses. He shares his insights and experiments at http://blog.inflinx.com.

Sudha Belida is a senior software engineer and technology enthusiast. She has more than seven years of experience working with Java and JEE technologies and frameworks, such as Spring, Hibernate, Struts, and AngularJS. Her interests lie in entrepreneurship and agile methodologies for software design and development. She has a master's degree in computational science from the University of Utah. In her free time, she likes to travel and enjoy the outdoor environment that Utah has to offer.

About the Technical Reviewer

Manuel Jordan Elera is an autodidactic developer and researcher who enjoys learning new technologies for his own experiments and creating new integrations. Manuel won the 2010 Springy Award—Community Champion and Spring Champion 2013. In his little free time, he reads the Bible and composes music on his guitar. Manuel is known as dr_pompeii. He has tech reviewed numerous books for Apress, including *Pro Spring, 4th Edition* (2014), *Practical Spring LDAP* (2013), *Pro JPA 2, Second Edition* (2013), and *Pro Spring Security* (2013).

Read his 13 detailed tutorials about many Spring technologies, contact him through his blog at http://www.manueljordanelera.blogspot.com, and follow him on his Twitter account @dr_pompeii.

Acknowledgments

This book would not have been possible without the support of several people, and we would like to take this opportunity to sincerely thank them.

Thanks to the amazing folks at Apress; without you, this book would not have seen the light of day. Thanks to Mark Powers for being patient and keeping us focused. Thanks to our development editor Chris Nelson for his insights and suggestions in making this book better. Thanks to Steve Anglin for his constant support and the rest of the Apress team involved in this project.

Huge thanks to our technical reviewer Manuel Jordan Elera for his efforts and attention to detail. His valuable feedback has led to many improvements in the book.

Finally, we would like to thank our friends and family for their constant support and encouragement.

Introduction

Introducing Gradle is a quick start-up primer on the Gradle build automation tool. The book starts by explaining the fundamentals behind Gradle and showing you how to set up and test Gradle on your local machine. It explains the basics of Groovy, the language for creating Gradle build scripts. It then delves deeply into concepts such as dependency management, projects, tasks, lifecycle phases, and plugins. It also discusses Gradle's support for multi-projects and publishing artifacts to local and remote repositories. Finally, it concludes with a discussion of continuous integration (CI) and a review of Jenkins support for Gradle.

How This Book Is Structured

Chapter 1 starts with a gentle introduction to Gradle. It discusses reasons for adopting Gradle, and it provides an overview of its two alternatives: Ant and Maven.

Chapter 2 focuses on setting up Gradle on your machine and testing the installation. It also provides an overview of different files/folders that come as part of the Gradle distribution, and it shows a simple Gradle build script.

Chapter 3 delves into Groovy language basics and reviews its language features needed to build Gradle scripts.

Chapter 4 discusses Gradle's two building blocks—project and tasks. You will learn how to create tasks and declare dependencies between those tasks. You will also review the lifecycle of a Gradle build.

Chapter 5 delves deep into Gradle's support for Java projects. You will learn about the Java and War plugins and use them to build and deploy Java and web applications. The chapter also provides in-depth coverage of Gradle plugins. You will also look at building a custom plugin.

Chapter 6 provides a detailed coverage of dependency management. You will learn about principles behind dependency management and look at Gradle's support for managing those dependencies. You will also learn about the different types of dependencies and how to resolve dependency conflicts.

Chapter 7 reviews the intricacies of Gradle's multi-project builds. You look at the two types of project structures—hierarchical and flat. You also learn how to declare common and project specific behavior in root and subproject build files.

Chapter 8 discusses Gradle's support for publishing artifacts. You learn about archives configuration for declaring artifacts produced by a project. You then install Nexus Maven repository manager and publish artifacts to the repository. You also learn about the configuration needed to deal with additional artifacts.

Chapter 9 reviews continuous integration (CI) flow and explores Jenkins, a popular open source CI server. You look at installing Jenkins and configuring the necessary plugins to run a sample project located on the GitHub repository.

Target Audience

Introducing Gradle is intended for developers and automation engineers who want to get started quickly with Gradle. This book assumes basic knowledge of Java. No prior experience with Gradle is required.

Downloading the Source Code

The source code for the examples in this book can be downloaded from `www.apress.com/9781484210321`. The source code is also available on GitHub at `https://github.com/bava/intro-gradle`.

Once downloaded, unzip the code and place the contents in the `intro-gradle` folder. The source code is organized by individual chapters. Each folder contains build scripts and project files corresponding to that chapter.

Questions

We welcome reader feedback. If you have any questions or suggestions, you can contact the authors at `Balaji@inflinx.com` or `Sudha@inflinx.com`.

CHAPTER 1

■ ■ ■

Getting Started

Traditional software development typically involves writing code, compiling code, running tests, and assembling an archive that finally gets deployed or distributed. As software projects became more complex, additional steps such as running static code analysis, conditional inclusions of resources, and running security scans have become part of the mainstream build and deployment process. Build automation tools allow you to automate these steps, which helps make builds repeatable and predictable. In this book, we will discuss and explore the features of Gradle, a popular build automation tool.

Gradle (http://gradle.org/) is the newest addition to the Java build project automation tool family. It is open sourced under Apache License 2.0 and its first version (0.7) was released in 2009, followed by version 2.0 in 2014. At the time of writing this book, version 2.7 is the current version of Gradle. Gradle has been gaining a lot of adoption as it draws on lessons learned from other existing build tools such as Ant and Maven. Several high-profile projects such as Android, Spring Framework, and Hibernate have migrated their build systems to use Gradle. Let's look at some reasons for Gradle's popularity.

Declarative Dependency Management

Most Java projects rely on other projects and open source frameworks to function properly. It can be cumbersome to download these dependencies manually and keep track of their versions as you use them in your projects. To make things more complicated, these dependencies might have their own dependencies (referred to as *transitive dependencies*) that need to be resolved and downloaded.

Gradle provides a convenient way to declare your project dependencies. It then automatically downloads those dependencies (along with transitive dependencies) and allows you to use them in your projects. This simplifies project dependency management greatly. It is important to note that you only tell Gradle the what and not the how.

1

Declarative Builds

Gradle uses a Groovy (http://groovy-lang.org/) based domain specific language (DSL—see https://docs.gradle.org/current/dsl/) for declaring builds. The DSL provides a set of language elements that can be easily assembled to create build scripts that are simple and clearly express their intent.

Build by Convention

Gradle provides sensible defaults and conventions for Java, Groovy, web, Scala, Android, and OSGi projects. For example, Gradle recommends that all the production source code for a Java project reside under the folder src\main\java. In the same way, it has recommendations for where the test code and resources should go. Additionally, default tasks get configured automatically for a Java project that would compile the code, and then run, test, and generate a JAR artifact.

Adhering to these conventions would make the build scripts very concise. However, you are not limited to follow these conventions. Since the Gradle's DSL is based on Groovy, it is easy to write Groovy code to tweak and deviate from these conventions.

Incremental Builds

Complex projects often run into slow build times as the build tool tries to "clean" and rebuild everything. Gradle addresses this problem by providing incremental builds that skip the execution of a task if neither the inputs nor the outputs have changed. For example, the JavaCompile task takes a set of Java source files as input and generates a set of class files. Gradle uses this information to check if the source files have changed and if no changes are detected, the task gets skipped.

Gradle Wrapper

Gradle Wrapper is simply a batch file (gradlew.bat) in the Windows environment and a shell script for Linux/Mac environments. When it runs, the wrapper script downloads and installs a fresh copy of Gradle runtime on the machine and executes a Gradle build. Gradle Wrapper makes it easy to spin up new continuous integration (CI) servers that can run builds without any additional configuration. The wrapper also makes it easy to distribute code and collaborate with others, as the recipients can easily build it.

Plugins

Gradle makes it easy to augment and customize its functionality through plugins. *Plugins* are distributable components that encapsulate reusable build and task logic. Using plugins, it is possible to support additional languages, create new tasks, or modify existing task functionality and extend build language by adding new keywords. With Gradle, you can easily create your own plugins, thereby enabling you to integrate tasks and workflows that are specific to your organization.

Open Source

Gradle is open source and costs nothing to download and use. It comes with rich online documentation and the support of an active community. Additionally, Gradle Inc. offers consulting and commercial support for the Gradle ecosystem.

Gradle Alternatives

Before you dig deep in to Gradle, take a look at couple of its alternatives—Ant + Ivy and Apache Maven.

Ant + Ivy

Apache Ant (http://ant.apache.org) is a popular open source tool for scripting builds. Released in 2000, it was the first among the "modern" build tools for the Java ecosystem. The framework is Java based and uses extensible markup language (XML) for its configuration. The default configuration file for Ant is the build.xml file.

Using Ant typically involves defining tasks and targets. As the name suggests, an Ant task is a unit of work that needs to be completed. Typical tasks involve creating a directory, running a test, compiling source code, building a web application archive (WAR) file, and so forth. A target is simply a set of tasks. It is possible for a target to depend on other targets. This dependency lets you sequence target execution. Listing 1-1 demonstrates a simple build.xml file with one target, called compile. The compile target has two echo tasks and one javac task.

Listing 1-1. Sample Ant build.xml File

```
<project name="Sample Build File" default="compile" basedir=".">
    <target name="compile" description="Compile Source Code">
      <echo message="Starting Code Compilation"/>
      <javac srcdir="src" destdir="dist"/>
      <echo message="Completed Code Compilation"/>
    </target>
</project>
```

Ant doesn't impose any conventions or restrictions on your project and it is known to be extremely flexible. This flexibility has sometimes resulted in complex, hard-to-understand and maintain build.xml files.

Apache Ivy (http://ant.apache.org/ivy/) provides automated dependency management, making Ant more joyful to use. With Ivy, you declare the dependencies in an XML file called ivy.xml, as shown in Listing 1-2. Integrating Ivy with Ant involves declaring new targets in the build.xml file to retrieve and resolve dependencies.

Listing 1-2. Sample Ivy Listing

```
<ivy-module version="2.0">
    <info organisation="com.apress" module="gswm-ivy" />
    <dependencies>
      <dependency org="org.apache.logging.log4j" name="log4j-api"
rev="2.0.2" />
    </dependencies>
</ivy-module>
```

Maven

Apache Maven is currently the most popular build automation/project management tool in the Java ecosystem. Released in 2004, Maven attempted to address many problems faced by Ant users. It adheres heavily to convention over configuration and introduced standard directory structure to projects. It also introduced declarative dependency management and automatically downloaded needed dependencies from external repositories.

Maven uses XML for providing project, dependency metadata, and build configuration. This information is provided in a pom.xml file defined at the root of the project. Listing 1-3 shows an example pom.xml file for a Java project.

Listing 1-3. Sample pom.xml File

```
<project xmlns="http://maven.apache.org/POM/4.0.0"
xmlns:xsi="http://www.w3.org/2001/XMLSchema-instance"
    xsi:schemaLocation="http://maven.apache.org/POM/4.0.0
    http://maven.apache.org/xsd/maven-4.0.0.xsd">
    <modelVersion>4.0.0</modelVersion>
    <groupId>com.apress</groupId>
    <artifactId>test-service</artifactId>
    <version>1.0.0-SNAPSHOT</version>
```

```
<dependencies>
    <dependency>
        <groupId>junit</groupId>
        <artifactId>junit</artifactId>
        <version>3.8.1</version>
        <scope>test</scope>
    </dependency>
</dependencies>
```

```
</project>
```

In this pom.xml file, the groupId, artifactId and version elements provide information about the project being built. The dependencies element indicates the artifact (JUnit in this case) on which the project depends.

Maven's convention over configuration, though helpful, can sometimes be too rigid and it's difficult to deviate from the conventions. Maven's use of XML is not very expressive and can become too restrictive for declaring complex build logic.

■ **Note**   To learn more about Maven, refer to *Introducing Maven* (http://www.apress.com/9781484208427) by Balaji Varanasi and Sudha Belida (Apress 2014).

Summary

Gradle greatly simplifies the build process and automates build management. This chapter provided a gentle introduction to Gradle and described the main reasons for adopting it. You also looked at Gradle's close peers—Ant + Ivy and Maven.

In the next chapter, you will learn about the set up required to get up and running with Gradle.

▩ ▩ ▩

CHAPTER 2

Setting Up Gradle

Gradle installation is an easy and straightforward process. This chapter explains how to install and set up Gradle using the Windows 7 and Mac operating systems. You can follow similar procedure with other operating systems. In addition to the basic Gradle installation and setup, this chapter includes installation prerequisites, an initial example script, and information about Gradle Help and IDE support

Installation Prerequisites

Before you get started with the Gradle installation, you need to make sure you have Java installed and configured correctly and then download the current version of Gradle.

Setting Up Java

To install Java, download the JDK (not just Java Runtime Environment [JRE]) from `www.oracle.com/technetwork/java/javase/downloads/index.html` and follow the installation instructions specified on that web page. Gradle requires version 6.0 or higher version of JDK. This book uses JDK 7. (The instructions work with Java 8, as well.)

Once the JDK is installed on your machine, point the `JAVA_HOME` environment variable to the JDK installation. For example, if you have the JDK installed under `c:\java\jdk1.7`, the `JAVA_HOME` value should be set to `c:\java\jdk1.7`. Then modify the `PATH` environment variable and append `%JAVA_HOME%\bin` to its end.

Without the `JAVA_HOME` variable, you'll see the `"JAVA_HOME not found in your environment"` build error.

Downloading Gradle

Before you begin the installation process, download the latest version of Gradle from the Gradle web site (`https://gradle.org/gradle-download/`). At the time of this writing, the latest version was 2.7. Download the Gradle 2.7 "Complete Distribution" file (`gradle-2.7-all.zip`) shown in Figure 2-1.

DOWNLOAD GRADLE

The latest release of Gradle is version 2.7, released on *14th September 2015.*

- Complete distribution (binaries, sources and offline documentation)
- Binary only distribution (no documentation or source code)
- Gradle source code (just the Gradle source code; not a usable Gradle installation)

Figure 2-1. *Gradle download options*

Installing Gradle

This section covers installing and testing Gradle on Windows and Mac OS X. The section also includes Gradle's JVM options and an overview of the distribution's file set.

Installing on Windows

Unzip the downloaded distribution to a local directory on your computer. It will create a folder named `gradle-2.7-all`. This book assumes that you have placed the contents of the `gradle-2.7` folder in the `c:\tools\gradle-2.7` directory, as shown in Figure 2-2.

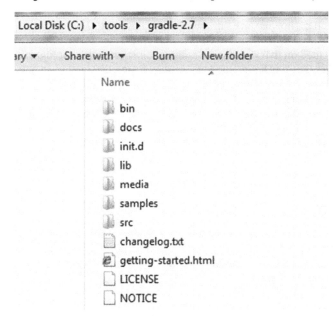

Figure 2-2. *Gradle install location*

The next step in the installation process is to add the GRADLE_HOME environment variable pointing to the Gradle installation directory—in our case that's c:\tools\gradle-2.7. Launch the Start menu and right-click the Computer option. Next, select System Properties followed by the Advanced System Settings. This will launch the window shown in Figure 2-3.

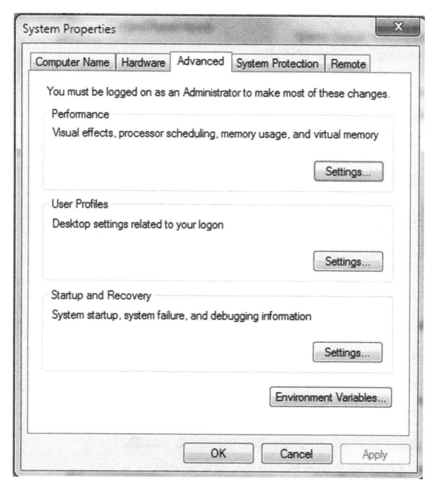

Figure 2-3. The System Properties window

9

Click the Environment Variables button, and then click New under System Variables. Enter the values shown in Figure 2-4 and then click OK.

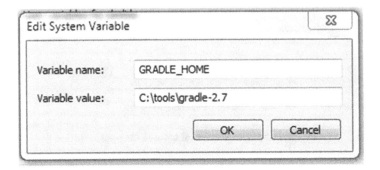

Figure 2-4. *Gradle Home system variable*

The final step in the process is to modify the Path environment variable so that you can run Gradle commands from the command line. Select the Path variable and click Edit. Add %GRADLE_HOME%\bin at the beginning of the Path value, as shown in Figure 2-5. Click OK. This completes the Gradle installation. If you have any open command-line windows, close them and reopen a new command-line window. When environment variables are added or modified, new values are not propagated to open command-line windows automatically.

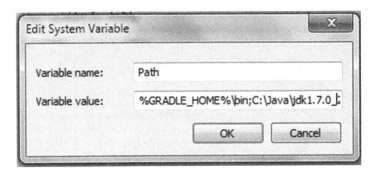

Figure 2-5. *Adding Gradle home location to the path variable*

Testing the Installation

Now that Gradle is installed, it's time to test and verify the installation. Open a command prompt and run the following command:

```
gradle -v
```

This command should output information similar to that shown in Figure 2-6.

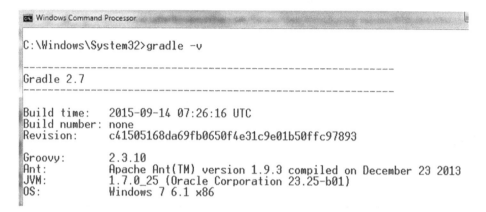

Figure 2-6. *Gradle version command*

The -v command-line option tells the path where Gradle is installed and what versions of Java, Ant, and Groovy it is using. You get the same results by running the expanded command gradle --version.

Installing on Mac OS X

Unpack the downloaded distribution and move the contents of the gradle-2.7-all folder under /Users/<<your_user_name>/tools, as shown in Figure 2-7.

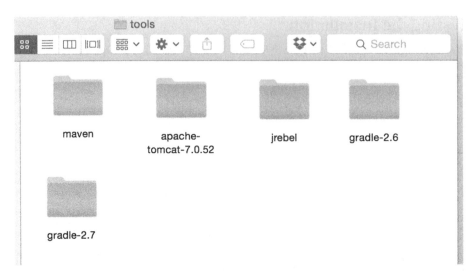

Figure 2-7. *Gradle installation location on Mac*

Launch a terminal to edit the initialization script `.profile` located in your home directory using this command:

```
nano ~/.profile
```

In the `.profile` file, add the following lines:

```
export GRADLE_HOME = /Users/<<your_user_name>/tools/gradle-2.7
export PATH=$PATH:$GRADLE_HOME/bin
```

Save the changes by pressing CTRL+O. Then exit the file by pressing CTRL+X. Run the `gradle -v` command to verify that the installation was successful.

Setting Gradle's JVM Options

Like every other Java application, Gradle shares the same JVM options set by the environment variable JAVA_OPTS. Especially in a complex project, chances are that you will run into OutOfMemory errors. This may happen, for example, when you are running a large number of JUnit tests or when you are generating a large number of reports. To address this error, increase the heap size of the Java virtual machine (JVM) used by Gradle. This is done globally by creating a new environment variable called GRADLE_OPTS. To begin, we recommend using the value -Xmx512m or -Xmx1024m.

Gradle Distribution

Gradle distribution contains several files and folders, as you saw in Figure 2-2 (see "Installing on Windows"). Table 2-1 provides a brief summary of those and their purposes.

Table 2-1. *Gradle Distribution Files and Folders*

Folder	Description
bin	Contains Gradle executables
docs	Contains user guide (HTML/PDF), Javadoc, Groovydoc and Gradle DSL references
init.d	Contains any scripts that needs to be run for each build
lib	Contains dependencies (JARs, plugins) that are needed for Gradle to run
media	Contains Gradle icons and logos
samples	Contains templates and examples of complex builds and integration with tools
src	Contains the source code for Gradle

Hello World Gradle Script

Now that you have successfully installed Gradle, you can create your first Gradle script that does nothing but simply outputs the text Hello world!!. When executing a build, Gradle by default looks for a build script named build.gradle. You begin by creating a folder called hello-world. Inside the folder, you create build.gradle file and then copy the code from Listing 2-1.

Listing 2-1. Hello World Task

```
task helloWorld << {
    println 'Hello world!!'
}
```

Open a command prompt and navigate to the hello-world directory. Then execute the helloWorld task using the command gradle helloWorld. You should see the Hello world!! output as shown here:

```
C:\apress\chapter2\hello-world>gradle helloWorld
:helloWorld
Hello world!!

BUILD SUCCESSFUL

Total time: 3.594 secs
```

Listing 2-1 uses Gradle's DSL to define the helloWorld task and add an action to print Hello world!! to the console. You can accomplish this using a closure (code inside curly braces {}) and Groovy's println method, which is similar to Java's System.out.println method. As you will explore in Chapter 4, Gradle tasks can contain multiple actions. The << is a shortcut operator that indicates the last action (in this case, printing to the console) to be executed for a task.

The build output includes the name of the task run and the execution time. It is possible to run the same build that just outputs the task's output. This is accomplished using the' -q flag as shown here:

```
C:\apress\chapter2\hello-world>gradle -q helloWorld
Hello world!!
```

Getting Help

You can get a list of Gradle command-line options by using the –h or -help options. Running the following command will produce output similar to that shown in Figure 2-8.

```
gradle -help
```

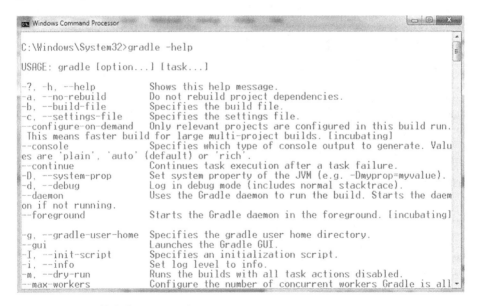

Figure 2-8. *Gradle help command*

Gradle GUI

In addition to providing a powerful command-line interface, Gradle comes with a graphical user interface for working with builds. Gradle's GUI can be launched using the --gui option. Figure 2-9 shows the Gradle GUI launched from the hello-world folder:

```
\chapter2\hello-world>gradle -gui
```

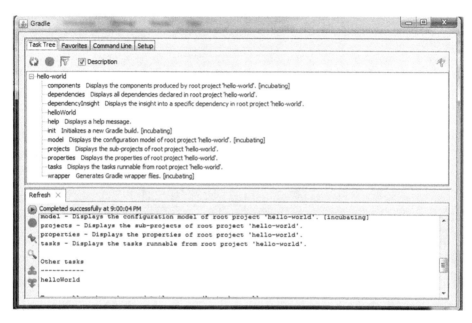

Figure 2-9. *Gradle GUI*

The Task Tree tab displays all the available tasks in the build.gradle file. You can execute a task in the Task Tree by simply double-clicking on a task name. The Favorites tab allows you to store frequently used Gradle commands. The Command Line tab, as the name suggests, allows you to type and run any Gradle commands that you would run using the command-line interface. The Setup tab allows you to change configuration options such as the project directory and log levels.

IDE Support

This book uses the command line to create and build sample applications. If you are interested in using an IDE, the good news is that all modern IDEs come with full Gradle integration.

Summary

This chapter walked you through the setup of Gradle on your local computer. You also learned the different files/folders that come as part of the Gradle distribution and looked at a simple Gradle build script.

In the next chapter, you'll learn fundamentals of the Groovy language.

CHAPTER 3

■ ■ ■

Groovy Language Primer

Gradle build scripts are written using Groovy. This chapter covers the basics of the Groovy programming language.

Groovy is a dynamic programming language that runs on the JVM. Groovy language is designed from the ground up to be source- and binary-compatible with Java. This compatibility allows Groovy classes to extend Java classes or leverage the vast array of Java frameworks and libraries. The 1.0 version of Groovy was released in January of 2007. The next major release—Groovy 2.0—was in July 2012. At the time of writing this book, the latest version of Groovy was 2.4. Groovy is open source and is distributed under the Apache 2.0 License.

Installing Groovy

Gradle comes with its own Groovy library and any existing Groovy installations will be ignored. In order to learn and tinker with Groovy, you need to install Groovy first. An external Groovy installation would allow you to get familiar with the language without messing up the Gradle installation. Follow these steps for installing Groovy:

1.   Download Groovy binaries from www.groovy-lang.org/ download.html.

2.   Extract the ZIP file and place the contents on your hard drive. For example,C:\tools\groovy-2.4.5.

3.   Create a new environment variable called GROOVY_HOME, pointing to the extracted location.

4.   Add GROOVY_HOME\bin to the PATH environment variable. For example, on a Windows machine, you would add %GROOVY_HOME%\bin.

5.   Once Groovy is successfully installed, run the groovy -v or groovy -version command on a command line to verify the installation. Figure 3-1 shows the output of a successful installation.

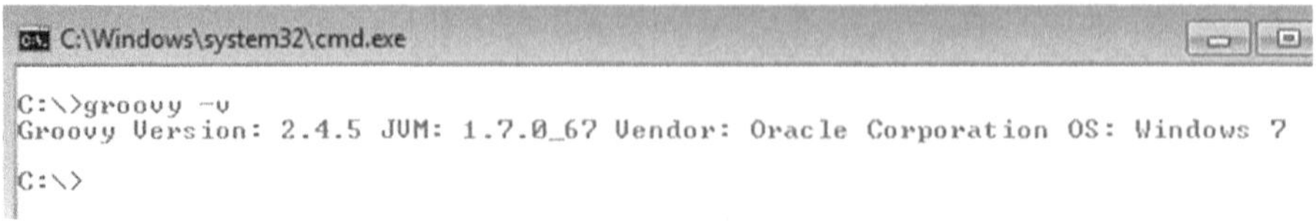

```
C:\Windows\system32\cmd.exe                                              [ - ] [ □ ]
C:\>groovy -v
Groovy Version: 2.4.5 JVM: 1.7.0_67 Vendor: Oracle Corporation OS: Windows 7
C:\>
```

Figure 3-1. *Groovy version command*

Running Groovy

Groovy provides a command-line tool called Groovy Shell or groovysh. It allows you to easily and quickly experiment with the language. To launch groovysh, open a command prompt/terminal and type groovysh. Once the shell finishes launching, you can start typing Groovy code and see it in action, as shown here:

```
C:\apress\intro-gradle>groovysh
Groovy Shell (2.4.5, JVM: 1.7.0_67)
Type ':help' or ':h' for help.
-------------------------------------------------------------------------
groovy:000> println 'Hello World'
Hello World
===> null
groovy:000>
```

You can exit the Groovy shell by running the command :exit or :quit. You can also run the :help command to list available shell commands or get details on an individual command.

Groovy also provides GroovyConsole—a GUI-based tool for executing Groovy code. To launch the GroovyConsole, simply double-click the groovyConsole.bat (for Windows) under the GROOVY_HOME\bin directory. Figure 3-2 shows GroovyConsole with an input area and an output area. The input area is where you enter Groovy code (such as println 'Hello World' shown in Figure 3-2). The Groovy code can be compiled and executed using the Script ➤ Run menu item or by choosing Run from the Action menu. The output of the execution is shown in the output area.

Figure 3-2. *GroovyConsole example*

Basic Groovy Language Features

This section covers Groovy syntax, data types (simple and collections), and closures. If you are interested in learning more about Groovy's language features, refer to the online documentation at `www.groovy-lang.org/single-page-documentation.html`.

Groovy Syntax

Groovy absorbs much of its syntax from Java and has added simplifications that make it an easy to use. One such simplification is dropping the semicolon requirement at the end of a line when the line contains only one statement. Similarly, methods with at least one parameter can be invoked without parentheses. The following two statements are valid in Groovy:

```
println ("Hello World");
println "Hello World"
```

Here are few more notable differences from Java:

- Methods and classes in Groovy are public by default.

- The `return` statement is optional in methods. If Groovy doesn't find a `return` statement, it returns the last evaluated expression.

- Checked exceptions need not be caught or declared. Groovy automatically wraps those exceptions as a `RuntimeException`.

- By default, the following packages are imported—`java.lang.*`, `java.util.*`, `java.util.regex.*`, `java.net.*`, `java.io.*`, `groovy.lang.*`, `groovy.util.*`, `java.math.BigDecimal`, and `java.math.BigInteger`.

Comments

Groovy comments have the same syntax as that of Java. Single-line comments start with // and multi-line comments start with /* and end with */. Groovydoc comments are similar to Javadoc comments and begin with /** and end with */.

Data Types

The Groovy language offers several data types such as numbers, strings, and complex data types such as lists and maps.

Strings

Groovy supports two types of strings—regular Java strings that are instances of `java.lang.String` and GStrings, which are instances of `groovy.lang.GString`. Regular Groovy strings are declared by surrounding sequences of characters with single, double, or triple quotes. Here are a few examples of `String` declarations:

```
String message = 'Hello World'
String processor = "Intel"
String multiLine = '''This text is on line one
    line 2 and
    line 3'''
String escapedExample = 'Bob\'s Burgers'
```

Triple quotes syntax allows you to place the text across line boundaries without having to split and concatenate it on each line. Groovy preserves the whitespace in a multi-line text declared using triple quotes. For example, the variable `multiLine` shown above will hold text containing whitespaces and newline characters. If you were to save that text in a database, it would be saved as shown:

```
This text is on line one
    line 2 and
    line 3
```

■ **Note**   Like Java, Strings in Groovy are immutable. If the contents of a string need to be changed, then it is recommended you use `StringBuilder` or `StringBuffer`.

GStrings are strings that are escaped using double quotes (or slashes //) and contain Groovy expressions with the ${...} syntax. When a GString is accessed, Groovy evaluates the expression and replaces the expression text with its value. An example of a GString is shown here:

```
String name = 'Luke'
String message = "Hello ${name}"
println message// This will print Hello Luke
```

When expressions are simple references to variables, the curly braces {} can be omitted. Hence, the `message` in the previous code can be rewritten as follows:

```
String message = "Hello $name"
```

■ **Note**   Languages such as Ruby and Perl have the concept of string interpolation, which is the ability to replace an expression in a string with its value. Hence, GStrings are often referred to as interpolated strings.

Groovy allows method calls, statements, and variable names inside the ${...} Groovy expressions. Using GStrings, you can easily create templates without needing an external templating engine. Here is an example that invokes the length() and toLowerCase() methods inside expressions:

```
String name = 'Luke'
String count = "${name.length()}"
println count
println "${name.toLowerCase()}"
```

Numbers

Groovy supports both integers and floating-point numbers. Unlike Java, Groovy doesn't offer primitive data types. Instead everything in Groovy is an *object*. This allows you to invoke methods on what looks like primitives as shown here:

```
8.toString()
4.times {
        // Run a task
}
7.next()
```

By default, integers in Groovy are instances of java.lang.Integer, java.lang. Long, or java.math.BigInteger. Groovy will automatically pick the smallest class to accommodate the integer's value. Here is an example:

```
println 90.class                    // Prints class java.lang.Integer
println 9999999999999999999.class   //Prints class java.math.BigInteger
```

Floating-point numbers by default are instances of java.math.BigDecimal:

```
println 9.0.class     //Prints class java.math.BigDecimal
```

It is always possible to override the default behavior by explicitly associating a type or using suffixes as shown here:

```
println 90l.class     // Prints class java.lang.Long
float foo = 9.0
println foo.class     // Prints class java.lang.Float
```

If Groovy doesn't support primitive types, then you might be wondering how basic arithmetic such as 2 + 3 or 10/2 using operators is possible. Groovy has overloaded the operators and the operators are actually method calls in Groovy. For example, 2 + 3 is equivalent to 2.plus(3). Since the operators are methods, if one of the operands is a null, then executing the operation would result in a NullPointerException.

■ **Note**   Unlike Java, Groovy performs floating-point division by default. For example, the operation 2/4 would result in 0.5. In Java, the same operation would result in o since Java detects both operands as integers and an integer division would be performed.

Declaring Variables

So far you have looked at declaring variables using data types. Groovy also provides the def keyword, which can be used for variable declaration when you are not sure or don't care about the variable data type. For example

```
def obj = 'a'
println obj.class     // Prints class java.lang.String
obj = 1.4
println obj.class     // Prints class java.math.BigDecimal
```

It is possible to omit the def keyword during variable declaration. Here is the previous code with def omitted:

```
obj = 'a'
println obj.class        // Prints class java.lang.String
obj = 1.4
println obj.class        // Prints class java.math.BigDecimal
```

Lists

Lists in Groovy are an ordered collection of items. By default, Groovy lists are instances of java.util.ArrayList and have the following declaration syntax:

```
list = [1, 2, 3, 4]
listWithDiffItems = [1, 3, 'String Item', 3.4]
```

As in Java, items in a list can be accessed using the get method. Groovy also provides a getAt method that, among other things, allows you to use negative indexes to access items starting at the end:

```
println list.get(1)      // Prints 2
println list.getAt(-1)   // Prints 4, the first element from last
```

Items can be added or removed using the add and remove methods. The each method can be used to iterate over the list items:

```
list.add 5
list.remove 0     // 0 is the index of the element to be removed
list.each { println it }
```

Note that he each method took a closure as its parameter. You will learn more about closures later in the chapter.

Maps

Maps in Groovy contain key/value pairs. By default Groovy maps are instances of java.util.LinkedHashMap and have the following syntax:

```
[key1 : value1, key2 : value2]
```

Here is an example of a map defined in Groovy:

```
map = [ "red" : 1 , "yellow" : 2, "green" : 3 ]
```

Elements in a map can be accessed in several ways. The most common approach is to use the "." notation. Here are some examples:

```
println map.red //Prints 1
println map["yellow"] // Prints 2
println map.get("green") // Prints 3
```

You can add new values to a map using the put method and iterate over values using the each method:

```
map.put "blue", 4
map.each { println "Key: ${it.key} and Value: ${it.value}" }
```

Notice the use of the ${} expressions in the each() method. Groovy evaluates these expressions and prints the key/value pairs.

Range

Groovy provides a range operator (..) to create a range of objects. For example, the following code defines a range of integers from 0 to 9:

```
def intRange = 0..9
println intRange.size()      // Prints 10
intRange.each {print it}     // Prints 0123456789
```

Closures

To put simply, a *closure* is a block of executable code. Closures in Groovy are instances of groovy.lang.Closure. Since closures are objects, they can be assigned to variables or passed around as parameters to methods. Since they contain code, closures can be executed. Closures are often referred to as *anonymous functions*.

Closures in Groovy can accept parameters and return values. The syntax for declaring closures is as follows:

```
{ list of arguments -> closure body }
```

Closures are enclosed by curly braces {}. The list of arguments are separated by commas (,) and the closure body contains one or more statements. The symbol -> separates the argument list from the body. If the closure doesn't have a return statement, the output of the last statement is returned. Here is an example of a closure that accepts one parameter of type String:

```
def greet = {String name -> "Hello ${name}" }
```

This closure can be invoked using the reference variable greet as shown here:

```
greet "Joe"
greet.call "Joe"
```

If a closure doesn't take any arguments, the list of arguments and the -> symbol can be omitted. Here is a very simple example without any arguments:

```
def greet = {"Hello"}
```

In the scenario when no arguments are declared, an untyped argument called it will be implicitly available to the closure body. Consider the following example, which makes use of the it argument:

```
def greet = {"Hello $it"}
```

When the greet closure is invoked with a parameter, such as "World", it would print Hello World. If the greet is invoked without a parameter, a null is passed.

```
def greet = {"Hello $it"}
greet "World"      // Prints Hello World
greet()            // Prints Hello null
```

Here are few more examples of closure definitions:

```
{ -> }                     // Empty Closure
{ a, b -> a + b }          // Closure with two untyped arguments
{int a, int b -> a + b}    // Closure with two arguments of type int
```

Closures can be passed as parameters to methods. In fact, the "List" and "Map" sections of this chapter showed how to pass the closure {print it} to the list or map's each method. The each method takes in a parameter of type groovy.lang.Closure and executes it for each item in a list or map. The closure accesses the item through the implicit it parameter.

Closures may access the variables declared within their scope. For example, if a closure is defined inside a method, it can access all the variables that the method has access to (parameters, local variables, class variables, etc.).

Summary

Groovy is the language of choice when working with Gradle. This chapter covered installing Groovy and using the Groovy shell and GroovyConsole. It reviewed the basics of Groovy and its supported data types. You learned that Groovy's GStrings allows you to include expressions, thereby making them suitable for templating. Finally, you learned about closures—blocks of code/functionality that can be passed around.

In the next chapters, you will take a deep dive into Gradle's tasks and start developing Gradle build scripts.

CHAPTER 4

■ ■ ■

Understanding Gradle Builds

Central to Gradle are two basic building blocks—projects and tasks. A Gradle build is made up of one or more projects and each project contains one or more tasks. This chapter reviews those two building blocks. You will review these building blocks and learn about the lifecycle phases associated with builds.

Projects

A *project* in Gradle is an abstract concept that represents an artifact that needs to be built. For example, a Gradle project could be a Java application that gets assembled into a JAR file. A Gradle project can also represent a piece of work that needs to be accomplished. For example, a Gradle project can be used to deploy an application.

For each project in the build, Gradle creates an instance of org.gradle.api.Project and associates it with the build script. This allows the build scripts to use Project's API to access properties and customize build behavior at runtime (for example, by creating new tasks or skipping existing tasks). Table 4-1 lists some of the commonly used properties and methods in the Project API.

Table 4-1. *Commonly Used Project API Properties and Methods*

Property/Method	Description
name	Name of the project and can be changed using the settings.gradle file. By default, the project directory name.
description	Description of the project. Typically set in the build.gradle file.
version	Project's version.
parent	Returns the parent project (if exists).
group	User-defined identifier indicating group or organization responsible for the project. For example, org.hibernate or org.springframework.
task	Overloaded method to create a new task.
dependencies	Configures dependencies for a project.
repositories	Configures repositories for a project.
defaultTasks	Configures the names of the default tasks to run for a project.

To access Project API's properties/methods, you can use the implicit variable project that Gradle associates with the build file. Listing 4-1 shows a Gradle build file named project-explicit.gradle located in the chapter4 folder. The build file contains code that sets Project's description and prints it on the console. Gradle will use the name chapter4 for the project object it creates for this build.

Listing 4-1. The project-explicit.gradle Example

```
project.description = "Hello World Project"
println "Project Description ${project.description}"
```

Notice that the code doesn't use the name build.gradle for this new build file. Gradle by default looks for a build.gradle file to run a build. It is possible to create build files with different names. In order to trigger builds using those files, you need to use the command line option -b or --build-file, followed by the file name. In this chapter, you will be working with a lot of examples and will be creating separate build files and running them using the -b option. Running the project-explicit.gradle build file would result in the following output.

```
chapter4>gradle -b project-explicit.gradle
Project Description Hello World Project
```

Gradle also allows you to leave out the project variable name when accessing Project API methods or properties:

```
description = "Hello World Project"
println "Project Description ${description}"
```

It is possible to define additional project-level properties using the syntax <<name>> =<< value>> inside an ext {} closure or using the shortcut ext.<<name>>=<<value>>. Listing 4-2 shows two additional properties—environment and outputLang—defined inside a new build file named project-add-properties.gradle.

Listing 4-2. The project-add-properties.gradle Example

```
description = "Hello World Project"
println "Project Description ${description}"
ext {
    outputLang = "English"
}
ext.environment = "local"
println "Output Language: ${project.outputLang}"
println "Environment: ${environment}"
```

Running this script will yield the following output. Since the properties were defined at the project level, you can access their values directly or use the `project` prefix.

```
chapter4>gradle -b project-add-properties.gradle
Project Description Hello World Project
Output Language: English
Environment: local
```

Tasks

Gradle projects are made up of one or more tasks that perform build steps. Tasks execute actions such as compile Java source code and generate classes or clean target folders. It is also possible for tasks to depend on other tasks. For example, the task that runs test cases is dependent on the task that compiles Java code. Corresponding to each task in the build file, Gradle creates an instance of `org.gradle.api.Task`. By default it would be `org.gradle.api. DefaultTask` class. Table 4-2 shows some of the commonly used task-related API properties and methods.

Table 4-2. *Commonly Used Task-Related API Properties and Methods*

Property/Method	Description
name	Name of the task.
description	Description of the task
group	The task group that the task belongs to. Task groups provide a way to logically group related tasks.
enabled	Decides if a task is enabled or disabled.
dependson	Configures task dependencies.
doFirst	Adds an action to the beginning of the task's action list.
doLast	Adds an action to the end of task's action list.
onlyIf	Runs a task only if the passed in closure returns true.

In the upcoming sections, you will be using these properties and methods to create tasks, add actions, and declare dependencies between tasks.

Creating Tasks

At the simplest level, creating a task just requires the task name:

```
task displayProperties
```

Although this task is perfectly valid, it doesn't actually do anything. For a task to do something meaningful, you need to add some actions to it. Gradle provides the doFirst and doLast methods for associating actions with a task. As the name suggests, actions added to the doFirst method end up at the beginning of the list of actions that get executed. Actions added to the doLast method reside at the end of the action list. Listing 4-3 shows the updated displayProperties task with actions added.

Listing 4-3. displayProperties with Actions

```
description = "Sample Description for Project"
task displayProperties {
    description = "Task to display properties"

    ext {
        taskProp1 = "Prop Val"
    }

    doFirst {
        println "Project Description: $project.description"
        println "Task name $name"
        println "Task Description: $description"
    }

    doLast {
        println "Task Property 1: $taskProp1"
    }
}
```

Listing 4-3 updated the description property of the project object and then updated the task's description property inside the task's closure. Gradle allows you to declare additional properties at a task level using an ext closure. Properties that are shared across tasks and other configuration elements are typically declared as project properties. For example, the version numbers of the dependent artifacts are typically declared as project properties (more about that in Chapter 6). Properties specific to a task are declared as task properties. In Listing 4-3 used the ext closure to declare a task property named taskProp1. The code also added three actions to doFirst method and one action to the doLast method. In the doFirst method, the $project variable prints project object's description to the console. Since name and description are task properties, you can access them directly to print their values.

Create a new build file named display-properties.gradle and copy the contents of Listing 4-3. Execute the displayProperties task and you should see the following output. As you can see, the actions inside the doFirst were executed first, followed by the actions inside the doLast block.

```
\chapter4>gradle -b display-properties.gradle displayProperties
:displayProperties
Project Description: Sample Description for Project
Task name displayProperties
Task Description: Task to display properties
Task Property 1: Prop Val

BUILD SUCCESSFUL

Total time: 4.046 secs
```

■ **Tip**   When executing a task in the command-line, you don't have to specify full task name. A camelCase task name can be run by abbreviating each word. For example, the displayProperties task can be run using the following shortcut: `gradle -b display-properties.gradle dP`.

For Gradle to execute task(s), you need to pass in the name of the task(s) as part of the Gradle command, as you saw in the previous execution. Gradle provides a way to define one or more default tasks that can be run when no other tasks are provided using the defaultTasks method. Listing 4-4 shows the use of defaultTasks method to define displayProperties as the default task.

Listing 4-4. displayProperties with Default Task

```
description = "Sample Description for Project"

defaultTasks 'displayProperties'

task displayProperties {
    description = "Task to display properties"

    // Content removed for brevity
}
```

Once you have the display-properties.gradle file updated with the defaultTasks code, you can trigger task execution using the gradle -b display-properties.gradle command.

Task Dependencies

Nontrivial builds typically have several tasks and often a task needs another dependent task to be finished before it can run. For example, before you can run the package task to assemble an artifact, you must run the task to compile sources. Similarly, before the compile task can run, it might need to run a task to clean the output folder. Gradle provides several ways to declare such task dependencies.

Listing 4-5 shows the task-dependencies.gradle build file, which contains three tasks—clean, compile, and package. This example takes two approaches to declaring dependencies. The dependsOn method makes compile task dependent on the clean task. To make package task dependent on compile, you have to use task's dependsOn property. In Gradle, package is a reserved word and to use it as a task name, you must pass it as a parameter to the task method. Also, notice the use of the << operator as a shortcut for the doLast method.

Listing 4-5. task-dependencies.gradle

```
task clean << {
    println 'Executing clean task'
}

task compile << {
    println 'Executing compile task'
}
compile.dependsOn 'clean'

task ("package", dependsOn : 'compile') << {
    println 'Executing package task'
}
```

Run the package task and you will see that the clean and compile tasks are executed prior to running the package task:

```
\chapter4>gradle -b task-dependencies.gradle package
:clean
Executing clean task
:compile
Executing compile task
:package
Executing package task

BUILD SUCCESSFUL
```

To determine the order in which tasks need to be run, Gradle creates a *Directed Acyclic Graph* or DAG. Each task to be executed becomes a node in the graph. Dependencies between tasks are used to create edges between nodes. Figure 4-1 shows a representation of the DAG for the tasks in Listing 4-5.

Figure 4-1. *Gradle's task DAG representation*

A DAG does not contain a directed cycle. In other words, it's not possible to start at a node, follow a sequence of edges, and come back to the same node. Hence, Gradle never executes a task that has been executed before.

Consider the scenario in Listing 4-6, where you have both tasks A and B dependent on a task C.

Listing 4-6. task-dependencies2.gradle

```
task A << { println 'In task A' }

task B << { println 'In task B' }

task C << { println 'In task C' }

A.dependsOn 'C'
B.dependsOn 'C'
```

Since Gradle creates a DAG for task execution, when tasks A and B run, Gradle runs task C only. Create a `task-dependencies2.gradle` file with contents of Listing 4-6 and run the following command to verify this:

```
\chapter4>gradle -b task-dependencies2.gradle A B
:C
In task C
:A
In task A
:B
In task B
```

Consider a different scenario, where task A depends on task B and task C, as shown in Listing 4-7.

Listing 4-7. task-dependencies3.gradle

```
task A << { println 'In task A' }

task B << { println 'In task B' }

task C << { println 'In task C' }

A.dependsOn 'B'
A.dependsOn 'C'
```

When task A is run, the dependsOn ensures that B and C are run prior to executing A. Create a task-dependencies3.gradle file with Listing 4-7 contents and execute task A. You should see the following output:

```
\chapter4>gradle -b task-dependencies3.gradle A
:B
In task B
:C
In task C
:A
In task A
```

dependsOn doesn't guarantee the order in which dependent tasks will run. In Listing 4-7 for example, no guarantees are made that task B will run prior to task C or vice versa. There may be occasions where you want to ensure that B runs prior to C, for example. To accomplish this, Gradle provides the mustRunAfter method. Listing 4-8 shows the modified version of the previous listing with mustRunAfter added.

Listing 4-8. task-dependencies4.gradle

```
task A << { println 'In task A' }

task B << { println 'In task B' }

task C << { println 'In task C' }

A.dependsOn 'B'
A.dependsOn 'C'
B.mustRunAfter 'C'
```

Create a task-dependencies4.gradle file with Listing 4-8 contents and run task A. You should see the tasks run in C, B, and A order, as shown here:

```
\chapter4>gradle -b task-dependencies4.gradle A
:C
In task C
:B
In task B
:A
In task A
```

Skipping Tasks

There are occasions where you want to skip the execution of a task. For example, you want to run certain tasks only in the development environment while skipping them in the test and production environments. To accomplish this, Gradle provides the onlyIf method, which accepts a closure. If the closure returns false, then the execution of the task is skipped.

Listing 4-9 shows a task that runs only in the nonproduction environment. The onlyIf closure checks the existence of a property called env and verifies if its value equates to Prod.

Listing 4-9. skip-task.gradle

```
task skipInProd {

    onlyIf {
        !project.hasProperty('env') || project.env != "Prod"
    }

    doLast {
        println 'Task execution complete'
    }

}
```

You can pass an external property to the Gradle build script using -Pname=value at the command line. Copy the contents of Listing 4-9 into a skip-task.gradle file and execute the skipInProd task with the -Penv=Prod command-line argument. You should see the task skip execution shown here:

```
\chapter4>gradle -b skip-task.gradle skipInProd -Penv=Prod

:skipInProd SKIPPED

BUILD SUCCESSFUL

Total time: 2.82 secs
```

Gradle provides another technique for skipping tasks through task's enabled property. By default, the enabled property is set to true. However, it is possible to programmatically toggle its value and thereby affect task execution. Listing 4-10 shows the skipInProd task rewritten using the enabled property.

Listing 4-10. Skipping task Using the enabled Property

```
task skipInProd {

    enabled = !project.hasProperty('env') || project.env != "Prod"

    doLast {
        println 'Task execution complete'
    }

}
```

Gradle Task Types

Earlier in the chapter, you learned that Gradle creates an instance of org.gradle.api.Task for each task it finds in the build file. By default, these tasks are instances of org.gradle.api.DefaultTask and thereby inherit DefaultTask's properties and methods. Gradle provides several out-of-the-box task types that your tasks can extend and thereby receive additional functionality, such as ability to create a ZIP archive or execute a Java program. This section reviews some of those out-of-the-box task types.

Zip

The Zip task allows you to create ZIP archives from a set of files/directories. Here's an example Zip task:

```
task archiveTask (type : Zip) {
    archiveName  'images.zip'
    from 'images'
    into "$buildDir/dist"
}
```

The archiveTask reads files/folders from the images directory, creates a ZIP file named images.zip, and places it in the build/dist folder.

Copy

The Copy task allows you to copy files from one or more sources to a destination directory. Here's an example Copy task:

```
task copyTask(type : Copy) {
    from 'src/config/dev.cert'
    from 'src/db'
    into 'dist'
}
```

copyTask would copy a single file called dev.cert and all the files in the src/db folder into a dist folder.

Exec

The Exec task allows you to execute a command-line process. An example is shown here:

```
task showWindowsVersion(type:Exec) {
  commandLine 'cmd', 'ver'
}
```

On a Windows machine, this task finds the Windows OS version. The commandLine property requires the full command line, including the executable and the arguments. However, you need to split the command string on spaces and provide split items in a comma-delimited fashion. Hence the command cmd ver is split and provided as cmd, ver.

Delete

The Delete task allows you to delete files or folders. The following task deletes two folders—libs and docs.

```
task cleanTask (type : Delete) {
    delete 'build/libs', 'build/docs'
}
```

Build Lifecycle

Every Gradle build goes through three distinct lifecycle phases:

1. **Initialization phase:** In this phase, Gradle identifies all the build.gradle files it needs to process. For a single project build, only one build file is identified. For multi-project builds (more on that in Chapter 7), Gradle tries to locate all possible build files associated with these projects. Once Gradle identifies the projects participating in the build, it will create an instance of org.gradle.api.Project corresponding to each project.

2. **Configuration phase:** In this phase, the build scripts for all identified projects are executed. It is important to remember that no actual task execution happens during this phase. Instead, Gradle constructs a DAG of tasks objects per project. Gradle also executes the configuration sections of all the tasks, including disabled tasks.

3. **Execution phase:** In this section, Gradle identifies the tasks that need to be executed and runs them in the right order.

To better understand the build lifecycle, consider the `build-phases.gradle` build script shown in Listing 4-11. The script contains two tasks—noActionTask and withActionTask. Both tasks contain Groovy code directly in the task's closure. Additionally, the withActionTask has code inside the doLast method.

Listing 4-11. build-phases.gradle

```
task noActionTask {
    description = "A task with no actions"
    println "I am in the configuration block of $name"
}

task withActionTask {

    println "I am in the configuration block of $name"

    doLast {
        println "performing an action in $name"
    }
}
```

During the configuration phase, Gradle executes the code specified directly in the task's closure. Once the configuration phase is complete, Gradle executes the actions inside doFirst and doLast in the execution phase. For example, running a command to list all tasks would execute initialization and configuration phases to produce the following output:

```
\chapter4>gradle -q -b build-phases.gradle tasks
I am in the configuration block of noActionTask
I am in the configuration block of withActionTask
```

---------------output truncated--------------------

Running the withActionTask would result in execution of both configuration blocks as well as the action in the doLast method. Here is the resulting output:

```
\chapter4>gradle -q -b build-phases.gradle wAT
I am a in the configuration block of noActionTask
I am a in the configuration block of withActionTask
performing an action in withActionTask
```

Summary

In this chapter, you learned about project and tasks, the two building blocks of Gradle builds. You learned that a task can contain one or more actions that are defined inside a doFirst or doLast blocks. It is possible for tasks to depend on other tasks and Gradle creates a DAG to ensure that tasks are executed in the right order. It also ensures that each task is executed only once. You looked at two techniques—onlyIf and enable—for executing or skipping tasks. Finally, you reviewed the three build phases of a Gradle build.

In the next chapter, you will use Gradle to build Java and web projects. You will also learn about Gradle plugins and build a custom plugin.

CHAPTER 5

■ ■ ■

Projects and Plugins

Gradle provides a standardized project structure for domains such as Java, Scala, and Groovy. It takes a build-by-convention approach and provides recommendations on where different parts of the project should reside. For example, Gradle suggests that all of the Java source code should be placed in the `src/main/java` folder and all the test code should reside in the `src/test/java` folder. This standardization makes it easy for developers to jump from one project to another. This chapter covers Gradle's build-by-convention features for Java projects.

Gradle follows a plugin-based architecture that makes it easy to augment and customize its functionality. It provides several out-of-the-box plugins that make it easy to build Java projects. Additionally, Gradle makes it easy to create custom plugins that can be shared with other developers. This chapter reviews the Gradle plugins and shows you how to develop a custom plugin that generates build numbers.

Introducing Plugins

Plugins in Gradle encapsulate reusable build, task, or configuration logic. Using plugins, it is possible to add new tasks, new DSL elements, or sensible defaults and therefore extend Gradle's functionality.

Gradle plugins are grouped into two types—script plugins and binary plugins. Script plugins, as the name suggests, are Gradle build scripts that can be included in other build scripts. Script plugins provide an easy way to modularize common build logic. These script plugins can reside on local file system or can be included from remote servers using this syntax:

```
apply from: 'reusable-build.gradle'
```

Script plugins residing on a remote server can be imported using the following syntax:

```
apply from: 'http://your_server.com/plugin_path/plugin_name'
```

Binary plugins encapsulate reusable build logic in classes that implement the `org.gradle.api.Plugin<T>` interface. These classes are typically bundles into JAR files but can also reside inside a build script or inside the project under the `buildSrc` folder. Binary plugins can be used inside a build script using the following syntax:

```
apply plugin: 'plugin_id'
```

The `plugin_id` is the unique identifier for the given plugin. Gradle-provided plugins have the short names such as `java` or `groovy`, while the community plugins typically use the fully qualified names such as `org.hibernate.gradle.tools`.

Java Projects

Gradle comes with several out-of-the-box plugins that simplify Java development. This section reviews the `java` plugin used for building JAR artifacts, followed by `war` plugin for developing web applications. You will also learn about the Javadoc plugin that can be used to generate API documentation.

Using the Java Plugin

The Java plugin allows you to compile Java code, run unit tests, and assemble a JAR artifact. To see the plugin in action, start by creating a new Java project called `hello-gradle` on your machine. Create a `build.gradle` file and add the following code to apply the Java plugin:

```
apply plugin: 'java'
```

As discussed in the previous section, this plugin adds a set of tasks and properties to the build. You can look at these tasks by running the `gradle tasks` command. A portion of the output is shown here:

\hello-gradle>gradle tasks
```
:tasks

Build tasks
-----------
assemble - Assembles the outputs of this project.
build - Assembles and tests this project.
buildDependents - Assembles and tests this project and all projects that
depend on it.
buildNeeded - Assembles and tests this project and all projects it depends
on.
```

```
classes - Assembles classes 'main'.
clean - Deletes the build directory.
jar - Assembles a jar archive containing the main classes.
testClasses - Assembles classes 'test'.

Documentation tasks
-------------------
javadoc - Generates Javadoc API documentation for the main source code.

Verification tasks
------------------
check - Runs all checks.
test - Runs the unit tests.
```

■ **Note**　All Gradle commands are executed using a command line/terminal in the folder containing the build.gradle file.

The output shows a number of new tasks cleanly grouped by the plugin. The tasks such as assemble and jar under the Build tasks group are used for building and packaging. Instead of running these tasks individually, you typically run the build task, which compiles, tests, and assembles the code by triggering the assemble and check tasks. The javadoc task under Documentation tasks is used to generate the Javadoc API documentation. The tasks under the Verification tasks group run unit tests.

In addition to these tasks, the Java plugin provides some guidance on where different parts of Java project's code should reside. Table 5-1 shows the recommended directories.

Table 5-1. *Gradle Recommended Directory Structure for Java*

Directory	Assets to Put
src/main/java	Java source that needs to go to production
src/main/resources	Resources such as configuration files (XML) and property files that need to go to production
src/test/java	Java test source code
src/test/resources	Resources used during the testing phase

■ **Note**　Experienced Maven users would notice that Java plugin's directory conventions match Maven's recommended Java project structure. It is important to remember that these conventions are just recommendations and Gradle makes it easy to change them according to your project's needs.

Based on these recommendations, let's create the src/main/java folders under the hello-gradle folder. Create a HelloGradle.java class with the contents shown in Listing 5-1.

Listing 5-1. HelloGradle Java Code

```
public class HelloGradle {

    public static void main(String[] args) {

        System.out.println("Hello Gradle!!");

    }

}
```

Now you are ready to build the code using the gradle build command. The output of running the command is shown here:

```
\hello-gradle>gradle build
:compileJava
:processResources UP-TO-DATE
:classes
:jar
:assemble
:compileTestJava UP-TO-DATE
:processTestResources UP-TO-DATE
:testClasses UP-TO-DATE
:test UP-TO-DATE
:check UP-TO-DATE
:build

BUILD SUCCESSFUL

Total time: 4.479 secs
```

Once the build is successful, open the hello-gradle folder in Windows Explorer and you will see a build folder created with the contents shown in Figure 5-1. The classes folder contains the compiled classes and the libs folder contains the assembled JAR file. The tmp folder contains temporary generated files, such as a manifest file.

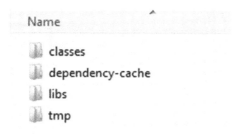

Figure 5-1. *Gradle build directory*

The output of the gradle build command shows the text "UP-TO-DATE" next to certain tasks. This text indicates that the particular task was skipped. Certain Gradle tasks declare a set of inputs to the task and a set of outputs from the task. For example, the compileJava task takes a set of Java files as input and produces a set of compiled classes as output. If Gradle determines that the inputs and outputs of a task have not changed since the last execution, it automatically skips the task execution. This feature is referred to as an *incremental build* and can considerably reduce build times in larger projects.

Jar Task

The Jar task provided by the Java plugin is responsible for assembling the JAR archive. The Jar task provides a number of properties that allow you to configure the generated artifact. One such property is archiveName. By default, the generated JAR file name will be the name of the project. In this case, the project name is hello-gradle and hence the build/libs folder contains a hello-gradle.jar file. The following code shows the configuration needed to change the generated JAR name to introducing-gradle.jar:

```
jar {
    archiveName = 'introducing-gradle.jar'
}
```

The Jar task also automatically adds a manifest file to the JAR file it creates. The manifest file typically contains information about the files packaged in a JAR file. To add new entries to the manifest file, you can use the Jar task's manifest property. Listing 5-2 shows the modified build.gradle file with configuration to add three new entries to the manifest file.

Listing 5-2. The New hello-gradle build.gradle File

```
apply plugin: 'java'

jar {
    manifest {
        attributes (
            'Main-Class' : 'HelloGradle',
            'Implementation-Title' : project.name,
            'Developer'  : 'Sudha Belida'
        )
    }
}
```

Run the gradle build command. After successful completion of the build, open the generated archive inside the builds/lib folder using a ZIP utility such as WinZip. The MANIFEST.MF file under META-INF folder should show these three new entries.

■ **Note**   For the build to produce an updated JAR with manifest entries, you might have to delete the existing hello-gradle.jar from the libs directory and re-run the build command.

Generating Javadoc

Javadoc is a great tool for documenting and understanding Java code. The Java plugin comes with the javadoc task, which can be used to automatically generate Javadocs. Before running the command, you should update the HelloGradle.java class by replacing its content with Listing 5-3.

Listing 5-3. HelloGradle with Javadoc

```
/**
* Class demonstrating Gradle Projects
*     @author Sudha
*/
public class HelloGradle {

    /**
    * Displays Hello Gradle!! to console
    *
    * @param args command line arguments
    */
    public static void main(String[] args) {
```

```
        System.out.println("Hello Gradle!!");

    }

}
```

Running the gradle javadoc command will yield an output as shown:

```
\hello-gradle>gradle javadoc
:compileJava
:processResources UP-TO-DATE
:classes
:javadoc

BUILD SUCCESSFUL

Total time: 6.39 secs
```

After successful command execution, the build folder will have a new docs folder with a javadoc subfolder containing the generated HTML files. The index.html file should look as shown in Figure 5-2.

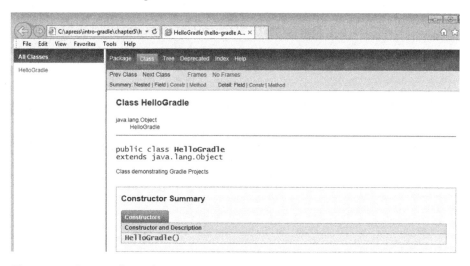

Figure 5-2. *Generated Javadoc*

Configuring the Default Layout

Gradle provides the notion of SourceSets, which represent a logical collection of source files. By default, the Java plugin provides the main and test SourceSets. However, when dealing with legacy projects, you might need Gradle to look for Java sources and other resource files in different locations. Listing 5-4 shows the use of sourceSets closure to change the default layout. The code indicates that the Java sources will be under the source/java folder and that the Java test cases will be under source/test folder.

Listing 5-4. Changing the Default Layout

```
apply plugin: 'java'

sourceSets {
    main {
        java {
            srcDir  'source/java'
        }
    }

    test {
        java {
            srcDirs = ['source/test', 'source/integration']
        }
    }
}
```

The srcDirs element can take a single directory or a set of directories as its value. Figure 5-3 shows an example project (hello-gradle2 in the downloaded source in the chapter5 folder) using the directory structure mentioned in the build.gradle file. It also shows the compiled classes in the build folder. Notice that the compiled classes are still created in the main and test folders. You can change the location of the generated classes using the output.classesDir config element.

```
├──build
│   └──classes
│       ├──main
│       │       HelloGradle.class
│       │
│       └──test
│               HelloGradleIT.class
│               HelloGradleTest.class
│
└──source
    ├──integration
    │       HelloGradleIT.java
    │
    ├──java
    │       HelloGradle.java
    │
    └──test
            HelloGradleTest.java
```

Figure 5-3. *Gradle project nondefault layout*

Creating Web Projects

Gradle provides a War plugin that extends the Java plugin and supports web application development and building WAR files. To see this plugin in action, create a folder named web-gradle. Create a build.gradle file inside the new folder and apply the web plugin as shown:

```
apply plugin: 'war'
```

This plugin provides the same directory conventions for storing Java classes as the Java plugin. Additionally, the War plugin expects all the static assets such as HTML, CSS, JS, Images, and dynamic assets such as JSP files to reside in the src/main/webapp folder. You should create the webapp folder under the src/main folder. Then create an index. html file and copy the contents from Listing 5-5.

Listing 5-5. The index.html File Contents

```html
<!DOCTYPE html>
<html>
    <head>
        <title>Hello World</title>
    </head>
    <body>
        <h1>Hello Gradle!!</h1>
    </body>
</html>
```

Now let's build the application using the gradle build command. You should see output similar to this:

```
\web-gradle>gradle build
:compileJava UP-TO-DATE
:processResources UP-TO-DATE
:classes UP-TO-DATE
:war
:assemble
:compileTestJava UP-TO-DATE
:processTestResources UP-TO-DATE
:testClasses UP-TO-DATE
:test UP-TO-DATE
:check UP-TO-DATE
:build

BUILD SUCCESSFUL

Total time: 5.415 secs
```

Gradle also provides plugins for running web applications inside an embedded servlet container such as Jetty and Tomcat. To configure Jetty, apply the Jetty plugin in build.gradle file as shown:

```
apply plugin: 'jetty'
```

Now, you can run the Jetty server by running the gradle jettyRun command. You will see this output:

```
\web-gradle>gradle jettyRun
:compileJava UP-TO-DATE
:processResources UP-TO-DATE
:classes UP-TO-DATE
> Building 75% > :jettyRun > Running at http://localhost:8080/web-gradle
```

To access the web page, launch a web browser and navigate to the URL: http://localhost:8080/web-gradle. You will see the web page as shown in Figure 5-4.

Hello Gradle!!

Figure 5-4. Index page

■ **Note**   It is possible to use embedded Tomcat for deploying web applications. Refer to the Tomcat plugin's GitHub page at `https://github.com/bmuschko/gradle-tomcat-plugin` for help with configuration.

War Task

The War task in the War plugin is responsible for assembling the WAR archive. By default, it performs the following actions:

- Copies compiled Java code to the WEB-INF/classes folder.

- Copies the content of src/main/webapp into the root of the WAR file.

- Copies dependencies in the runtime configuration to the WEB-INF/lib folder.

The War task provides several properties and methods that can be used to customize the generated artifact. The following code showcases some of these configuration options:

```
war {
    archiveName 'new-archive.war'
    webXml file ('src/config/web.xml')
    from 'src/media/images'
}
```

This configuration renames the generated artifact name to new-archive.war. It then configures the War task to use web.xml file located in the src/config folder. Finally, the task is configured to add the contents in the src/media/images folder to the root of the WAR file. With a War plugin, the contents of the WAR file by default are located

51

in src/main/webapp. It is important to remember that this configuration only appends the content from the images folder to the WAR file. If you want the War task to override the default behavior and look for contents elsewhere, say src/WebContent, you need to change the war plugin's webAppDirName property:

```
apply plugin: 'war'
apply plugin: 'jetty'

webAppDirName = 'src/WebContent'
```

Writing a Custom Plugin

Gradle makes it very easy to build custom binary plugins. You simply need to create a class that implements the org.gradle.api.Plugin<T> interface. The plugin class and its associated code can reside in one of the following three locations:

- **Build script:** The plugin source code can be directly embedded into the build script. This approach limits the reuse value of the plugin as the plugin is not visible outside the build script.

- **buildSrc project:** Plugin code that resides under the buildSrc project is automatically compiled and is made available in the build script's classpath. This plugin is also not visible outside the build and hence doesn't provide reuse outside the project.

- **Stand-alone project:** Plugin code can be bundled as a JAR file that can then be included in the build script's classpath. This approach provides the highest reuse value but also requires separate project and build infrastructure.

In the next sections, you will build a simple plugin with a single task that prints "Hello Gradle Plugin" to the console and a more complex plugin that generates a build number. You will take the buildSrc project approach for building the simple plugin. Gradle plugins can be written in any language that can compile to byte code. You will initially use Java to create the simple plugin followed by an example using Groovy. You will be using the stand-alone project approach for building the complex plugin.

Creating a Java Plugin

You'll begin your Hello Gradle Plugin development by creating a buildSrc folder inside the hello-gradle folder. To house Java code, underneath buildSrc, create the subfolders src/main/java. The directory structure should resemble the structure shown in Figure 5-5.

```
─hello-gradle
 │    build.gradle
 │
 ├───buildSrc
 │     └──src
 │         └──main
 │             └──java
 └──src
     └──main
         └──java
             HelloGradle.java
```

Figure 5-5. *The buildSrc Directory Structure*

The next step is to create a task that outputs "Hello Gradle Plugin" to the console. Create a GreetTask.java file under the buildSrc folder and copy the contents of Listing 5-6.

Listing 5-6. GreetTask.java Contents

```
import org.gradle.api.DefaultTask;
import org.gradle.api.tasks.TaskAction;

public class GreetTask extends DefaultTask {

    @TaskAction
    public void greetAction() {
        System.out.println("Hello Gradle Plugin");
    }

}
```

The easiest way to create a custom task in Gradle is to extend org.gradle.api. DefaultTask, which itself implements the org.gradle.api.Task interface. For the task to perform an action, you have to create the greetAction method with the System.out. println statement, which writes the message to the console. For Gradle to treat this method as an action to execute, you must annotate it with @TaskAction.

The next step is to write the plugin class itself. Create the HelloPlugin.java class in the buildSrc folder and copy the contents of Listing 5-7 into it.

Listing 5-7. The HelloPlugin.java Contents

```java
import org.gradle.api.Plugin;
import org.gradle.api.Project;
import java.util.Map;
import java.util.HashMap;

public class HelloPlugin implements Plugin<Project> {
    @Override
    public void  apply(Project project) {
        project.getTasks().create("greet", GreetTask.class);
    }
}
```

A Gradle plugin is created by implementing the org.gradle.api.Plugin<T> interface. The Plugin interface contains one method named apply(Project) that the plugin classes must implement. Gradle begins the plugin execution by invoking its apply method. Hence, you register the GreetTask inside the apply method using the passed-in Project argument. You do this using the create method to create a task and add it to the Project task container. The create method takes the name of the task being created along with the task class.

This concludes the plugin development. To use this plugin, add the following code to build.gradle file:

```
apply plugin: HelloPlugin
```

Now let's use the plugin and run the greet task using the command gradle greet. You should see the text "Hello Gradle Plugin" in the output, as shown here:

```
\hello-gradle>gradle greet
:buildSrc:compileJava
:buildSrc:compileGroovy UP-TO-DATE
:buildSrc:processResources UP-TO-DATE
:buildSrc:classes
:buildSrc:jar
:buildSrc:assemble
:buildSrc:compileTestJava UP-TO-DATE
:buildSrc:compileTestGroovy UP-TO-DATE
:buildSrc:processTestResources UP-TO-DATE
:buildSrc:testClasses UP-TO-DATE
:buildSrc:test UP-TO-DATE
:buildSrc:check UP-TO-DATE
:buildSrc:build
:greet
Hello Gradle Plugin

BUILD SUCCESSFUL

Total time: 5.725 secs
```

Creating a Groovy Plugin

This section recreates the Java HelloPlugin using Groovy language. To start, create a groovy folder in the buildSrc/src/main folder. The resulting folder structure is shown in Figure 5-6.

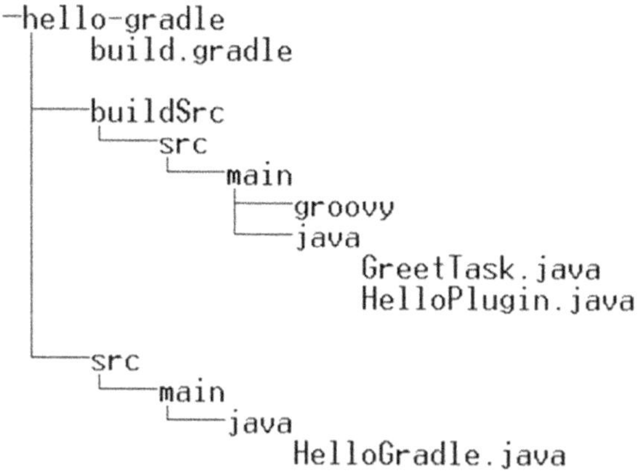

```
─hello-gradle
    │   build.gradle
    │
    ├──buildSrc
    │   └──src
    │       └──main
    │           ├──groovy
    │           └──java
    │                   GreetTask.java
    │                   HelloPlugin.java
    │
    └──src
        └──main
            └──java
                    HelloGradle.java
```

Figure 5-6. *The Groovy Plugin Directory Structure*

In the groovy folder, create the HelloPlugin2.groovy file and copy the contents of Listing 5-8.

Listing 5-8. HelloPlugin2 Using Groovy

```groovy
import org.gradle.api.Plugin;
import org.gradle.api.Project;

class HelloPlugin2 implements Plugin<Project> {
@Override
    void apply(Project project) {

        project.task('greet2') << {
            println 'Hello Gradle Plugin2'
        }

    }
}
```

The HelloPlugin2 implements the Plugin interface like Java's HelloPlugin class. In the apply method, you use the Project instance to create a new task named greet2. You also add an action to the task's doLast method using the << shortcut notation. The action closure code prints the text "Hello Gradle Plugin2" to the console.

Apply the newly created plugin using this statement:

```
apply plugin: HelloPlugin2
```

Run the gradle greet2 command to use the plugin. The output should be as shown here:

```
\hello-gradle>gradle greet2
:buildSrc:compileJava UP-TO-DATE
:buildSrc:compileGroovy UP-TO-DATE
:buildSrc:processResources UP-TO-DATE
:buildSrc:classes UP-TO-DATE
:buildSrc:jar UP-TO-DATE
:buildSrc:assemble UP-TO-DATE
:buildSrc:compileTestJava UP-TO-DATE
:buildSrc:compileTestGroovy UP-TO-DATE
:buildSrc:processTestResources UP-TO-DATE
:buildSrc:testClasses UP-TO-DATE
:buildSrc:test UP-TO-DATE
:buildSrc:check UP-TO-DATE
:buildSrc:build UP-TO-DATE
:greet2
Hello Gradle Plugin2

BUILD SUCCESSFUL

Total time: 5.451 secs
```

It is also possible to run both greet and greet 2 tasks using the command gradle greet greet2. You should see this output if you do so:

```
:buildSrc:build UP-TO-DATE
:greet
Hello Gradle Plugin
:greet2
Hello Gradle Plugin2
```

Creating a Stand-Alone Project Plugin

In the previous section, you built a simple plugin with source code residing in the buildSrc folder of the project. This approach is not very modular as the plugin can't be reused beyond the project where it is defined. The stand-alone project approach allows you to create a plugin that is packaged into a JAR file and can be easily distributed and reused by any number of projects. To better understand this plugin-development approach, you will create a more realistic plugin.

Plugin Background

Software projects typically have version numbers that are expressed using three numbers separated by periods:

```
<major-version>.<minor-version>.<patch/incremental-version>
```

As the naming convention suggests, the major versions are generally incremented for major feature changes that are usually not backward compatible. Minor versions are incremented when implementing minor features or major bug fixes. Finally, the patch/incremental versions are incremented for minor bugs, text changes, etc. This convention follows the "Semantic Versioning 2.0.0" guidelines described at http://semver.org/.

During development, it is possible for development teams to create multiple builds of the same source code and deploy them for testing or sharing with other developers. These builds will all have the same version number. In order to distinguish these builds individually, you typically use another number called the *build number*. Some software teams follow the convention of appending this build number to the version:

```
<major-version>.<minor-version>.<patch/incremental-version> .<build-number>
```

Other teams would simply add the build number to the generated JAR's manifest or display it on the application's UI. Here are some example versions with build number:

> 1.0.0.56
>
> 3.3.9.25BLR48
>
> 6.1.0-20151123154556

Build numbers can be obtained from a variety of sources—commit numbers from source code check-ins or build timestamps or continuous integration (CI) server-generated numbers, and so on. In this section, you will create a Gradle plugin that generates random build numbers.

Plugin Configuration

To keep things manageable for the book, the build number plugin generates two types of values—a numeric value based on the timestamp or an alphanumeric value. Listing 5-9 shows a hypothetical build.gradle configuration to use this plugin.

Listing 5-9. Build Number Plugin Example Usage

```
apply plugin: 'build-number-plugin'

buildNumber {
    numberType = 'alphanumeric'
    alphaNumLength = 5
}
```

The plugin provides a buildNumber configuration block that allows the plugin user to set the build number type—alphanumeric or timestamp. The user can use the alphaNumLength property to dictate the number of characters in the generated alpha numeric string.

Once the plugin is configured, the generated build number can be accessed in the build.gradle file using buildNumber.value.

■ **Note**   There are a few open source Gradle plugins available that generate build numbers from other sources such as Git/SVN and provide more bells and whistles. You can check out one such plugin at https://github.com/GeoNet/gradle-build-version-plugin.

Plugin Development

You'll begin the plugin development by creating a Groovy project. Create a folder called build-number-plugin on your file system followed by the subfolders shown in Figure 5-7.

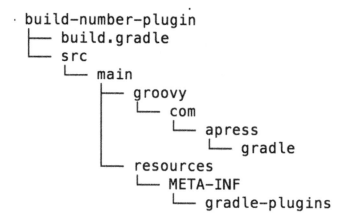

Figure 5-7. *Stand-alone project directory structure*

The next step is to populate the build.gradle file with dependencies and configuration needed for a plugin project. Listing 5-10 shows the contents of the build. gradle file.

Listing 5-10. The build.gradle file for the Build Number Plugin

```
apply plugin: 'groovy'

group = 'com.apress.gradle'
version = '1.0.0'

dependencies {
    compile gradleApi()
}

uploadArchives {
    repositories {
        flatDir { dirs "../repo" }
    }
}
```

Since you are dealing with a Groovy project, you must begin the build.gradle file by applying the Groovy plugin. Gradle artifacts are identified using three coordinates (more on this in Chapter 6):

- The group indicating the organization responsible for the project
- The name of the artifact
- The version of the artifact

In the build.gradle file, you use com.apress.gradle and 1.0.0 as group and version values. Since you didn't specify the name, Gradle uses the name of the project folder as the artifact name. The dependencies section of the file is used to provide Gradle the external libraries and frameworks the plugin project requires for compilation and testing purposes. In this case, you use the gradleApi() to pull in Gradle API used by custom plugin and task classes.

■ **Note**   In next the chapter, you will be taking a deeper dive into dependency management and Gradle's support for pulling in external dependencies

---

Finally, you use the uploadArchives method to upload or publish the generated plugin to a repository. The flatDir method is configured to publish the packaged plugin to a repo folder that exists at the same level as build-number-plugin (the project) on the file system.

■ **Note**   Generated artifacts can be shared with other developers/teams by publishing to central/common artifact repositories. Chapter 8 deals with artifact publishing in detail.

Plugin Extensions

The next step in developing the plugin is to make the plugin configuration in the user's build.gradle (Listing 5-9) available to the custom plugin. One way to achieve this is through extension objects. Every Gradle project has an instance of org.gradle.api.plugins.ExtensionContainer that keeps track of settings and properties passed to plugins. To store this data and pass it back and forth, you need to register one or more Java/Groovy beans (referred to as *extension objects*) to this container.

Listing 5-11 shows BuildNumberExtension.groovy class in the src/main/groovy/com/apress/gradle folder, which will act as an extension model for the build number plugin. It contains the numberType and alphaNumLength properties, which will hold the inputs to plugin. It also contains the value property that allows the plugin/task to make a build number available to the build.gradle file.

Listing 5-11. BuildNumberExtension.groovy Class

```
package com.apress.gradle;

class BuildNumberExtension {
    String numberType;
    int alphaNumLength;

    String value;
}
```

Plugin Task

In the "buildSrc" approach (Listing 5-8), you combined plugin code with task code. For real-world plugins, it makes sense to cleanly separate plugin code from code that executes actions. Hence, create the BuildNumberTask.groovy file in the src/main/groovy/com/apress/gradle folder and copy the contents of Listing 5-12.

Listing 5-12. BuildNumberTask Code

```
package com.apress.gradle;

import org.gradle.api.DefaultTask
import org.gradle.api.tasks.TaskAction

class BuildNumberTask extends DefaultTask {

    @TaskAction
    def generateBuildNumber() {
        String numberType = project.buildNumber.numberType
        int alphaNumLength = project.buildNumber.alphaNumLength

        def buildNumber;

        if("alphanumeric".equals (numberType)) {
            buildNumber = getAlphaNumString(alphaNumLength)
        }
        else if ( "timestamp".equals (numberType) ) {
            buildNumber = System.currentTimeMillis()
        }

        project.buildNumber.value = buildNumber;
    }

    def getAlphaNumString(length) {
        String uuid = UUID.randomUUID().toString()
        uuid.take(length)
    }
}
```

The @TaskAction on the generateBuildNumber() method inside BuildNumberTask indicates the method that Gradle needs to invoke to execute an action. The generateBuildNumber() implementation reads user-configured numberType and alphaNumLength values using buildNumber extension object. It then invokes the System.currentTimeMillis() or getAlphaNumString() utility method to generate the actual build number. The generated build number is then assigned to buildNumber's value property. This makes the build number available to the user's build.gradle file.

Plugin Class

The final piece to the implementation is the Plugin class that ties everything together. Listing 5-13 shows the BuildNumberPlugin class code located under the src/main/groovy/com/apress/gradle folder. Inside the apply() method, you use the create method to add the buildNumber extension object to the project. The create method takes a name and the model class as its parameters. This name, buildNumber, must match the name of the configuration closure block that the user will be using to provide inputs (buildNumber in Listing 5-9). It must also match the name that the task class (Listing 5-12) uses to retrieve configuration values.

Listing 5-13. BuildNumberPlugin Class

```
package com.apress.gradle;

import org.gradle.api.Plugin;
import org.gradle.api.Project;
import org.gradle.api.Task;

class BuildNumberPlugin implements Plugin<Project>  {

    void apply(Project project) {
        project.extensions.create('buildNumber', BuildNumberExtension)
        Task buildnumberTask = project.task('buildnumbertask', type:
BuildNumberTask)
        project.tasks['jar'].dependsOn buildnumberTask
    }
}
```

In the apply() method, you then add a task of type BuildNumberTask. The name buildnumbertask doesn't carry any special significance. However, you should strive to give a meaningful name as it gets displayed in the console and debug output. Finally, you make the Jar task depend on the buildnumberTask so that a build number is available to the build script before a JAR is generated.

Short Plugin Name

Plugins by default are referred to by their fully qualified class names. It is however possible to give your plugins short, easy-to-use, names. You do this by creating a properties file in the src/main/resources/META-INF/gradle-plugin folder. The name of the properties file becomes the plugin's short name.

Since this plugin deals with build numbers, you could call the plugin build-number-plugin. To accomplish this, create a build-number-plugin.properties file under the gradle-plugin folder. Inside the file, you simply create a property with the key implementation-class and the fully qualified plugin class as its value:

```
implementation-class=com.apress.gradle.BuildNumberPlugin
```

Plugin Packaging

This concludes the plugin implementation. The next step is to build an archive and publish it to the local file repository. To achieve this, use the command line to navigate to the `build-gradle-plugin` folder and run the command `gradle uploadArchives`. You should see this output:

```
\build-number-plugin>gradle uploadArchives
:compileJava UP-TO-DATE
:compileGroovy
:processResources UP-TO-DATE
:classes
:jar
:uploadArchives

BUILD SUCCESSFUL
```

■ **Note**   You will learn more about the `uploadArchives` command in Chapter 8.

Upon successful execution, you should see the `build-number-plugin-1.0.0.jar` file in the repo folder. As mentioned earlier, repo should be located at the same level as the `build-gradle-plugin` folder.

Consuming the Plugin

To consume the newly created plugin, create a new Gradle project named `plugin-consumer`. In this project, you add the plugin's build number to the generated JAR's `MANIFEST.MF` file.

To begin, create the `plugin-consumer` folder on your file system, next to the repo and `build-gradle-plugin` folders.

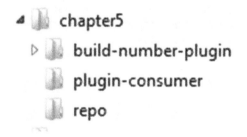

Figure 5-8. *Project directory structure*

Then create a build.gradle file for the plugin-consumer project. Since this is a Java project that generates a JAR artifact, apply the Java plugin. You also need to apply and configure the build-number-plugin, as shown here:

```
apply plugin: 'java'
apply plugin: 'build-number-plugin'

buildNumber {
    numberType = 'alphanumeric'
    alphaNumLength = 5
}
```

The next step is to add the plugin JAR file to the build script's classpath so Gradle can find the plugin classes. You accomplish this using a buildscript block:

```
buildscript {
    repositories {
        flatDir {
            dirs '../repo'
        }
    }
    dependencies { classpath 'com.apress.gradle:build-number-plugin-1.0.0' }
}
```

Finally, you use the doFirst method on the jar task to add a new manifest entry, as shown here:

```
jar.doFirst {
    manifest {
        attributes('Build-Number': project.buildNumber.value)
    }
}
```

You are now ready to generate the consumer plugin. Using a command line, navigate to the plugin-consumer folder and run the gradle build command. In the output, you should see the buildnumbertask getting triggered followed by Java plugin's task (compileJava, jar, etc.) execution. The output should look as follows:

```
\plugin-consumer>gradle build
:buildnumbertask
:compileJava UP-TO-DATE
:processResources UP-TO-DATE
:classes UP-TO-DATE
:jar
:assemble
:compileTestJava UP-TO-DATE
:processTestResources UP-TO-DATE
:testClasses UP-TO-DATE
```

```
:test UP-TO-DATE
:check UP-TO-DATE
:build
```

BUILD SUCCESSFUL

Upon successful completion of the build, navigate to the `plugin-consumer\build\` `libs` folder. Using a ZIP utility such as WinZip or WinRAR, open `plugin-consumer.jar` and open the `MANIFEST.MF` file under `META-INF`. You should see a `Build-Number` entry containing alphanumeric text, similar to Figure 5-9.

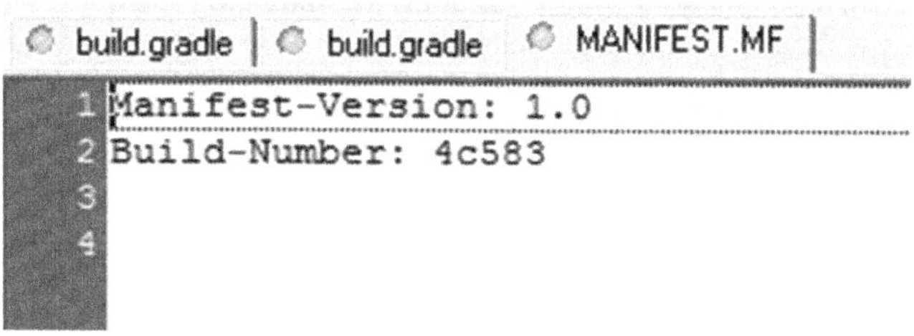

Figure 5-9. *Build number in the MANIFEST file*

To generate build numbers using a timestamp, replace the `buildNumber` configuration block in `build.gradle` file with this code:

```
buildNumber {
    numberType = 'timestamp'
}
```

Run the command `gradle clean build` and it should delete the existing JAR file and generate a new one. Upon successful build execution, you should see a timestamp-based build number in the generated manifest file.

This concludes the stand-alone project-based plugin development. You can publish this plugin to an internal Maven repository and make it available to rest of the development team. You can also publish it to Gradle Plugin Portal. The Gradle Plugin Portal at `https://plugins.gradle.org/` hosts numerous open source plugins contributed by developers across the world. The portal allows you to search for plugins you need and displays the necessary configuration to use those plugins. You can follow the instructions for the submission process at `https://plugins.gradle.org/docs/submit`.

Summary

Gradle greatly simplifies building of Java projects using plugins that provide tasks and sensible defaults. This chapter reviewed the java plugin that compiles Java code, runs unit tests, and assembles JAR archives. You then used the javadoc plugin to generate API documentation. The war plugin allows you to build and package web applications.

Gradle also provides excellent support for building custom plugins. You learned that there are three ways to package custom plugins—build scripts, use a buildSrc directory, and create a stand-alone project. You learned the basics of creating a simple Java and Groovy plugin using the buildSrc approach. You then built on those concepts to develop a plugin using a stand-alone project approach.

In the next chapter, you will read all about Gradle's support for managing dependencies and interacting with various artifact repositories.

CHAPTER 6

■ ■ ■

Dependency Management

Software projects are rarely built in isolation. They either depend on internal projects or other open source libraries. This chapter looks at how Gradle helps you effectively manage these dependencies. You will learn about the different types of dependencies, as well as learn how to group dependencies and resolve dependency conflicts. You will also review repositories that store artifacts.

Declarative Dependency Management

Consider the scenario where you want to use Logback (http://logback.qos.ch) in your application for logging. A straightforward approach is to download the logback.jar file from Logback web site and add it to your project. This used to be a pretty common behavior when using IDE or ANT for building projects. However, there are few issues with this approach:

- The downloaded JAR file might depend on a few other libraries. Such dependencies are referred to as *transitive dependencies*. To make things more difficult, transitive dependencies might have their own dependencies. You need to spend time figuring out all those dependencies and downloading them for use in your project.

- There could be version conflicts with transitive dependencies. Let's say your project depends on JAR A and B. Now if A depends on 1.0.0 version of JAR C and B depends on version 2.0.0 of C, you need to manually resolve this conflict.

- Downloaded JAR files must be checked into a Version Control System or placed on a shared drive so that the project can be built on other developer machines or on a Continuous Integration server. Checking JAR files in to VCS is not considered a best practice. This approach especially makes it hard when dealing with frequently changing working copies (referred to as *snapshot* versions in Maven).

- Upgrades become really difficult and you have to repeat this manual process all over again.

- It becomes hard to share internally developed JAR files across teams.

To address these inherent problems with ANT, Maven came up with declarative dependency management. With this approach, you tell the Maven what you need, typically in an external configuration file. Maven will automatically figure out where and how to get those dependencies and hand them over to your project. Later, Ant provided integration with another dependency management tool called Apache Ivy. Gradle provides its own dependency management implementation but does support the Maven and Ivy repositories.

Figure 6-1 provides a high level view of Gradle's dependency management. Gradle interacts with repositories to retrieve dependencies and associated metadata. Repositories that are accessed over the web are considered remote and are typically maintained by third parties. Gradle can also interact with repositories that exist on the local machine as well as directories containing JAR files. Once dependencies are obtained, Gradle stores them in a cache. By default, the cache is located at <<USER_HOME>>/.gradle on your local machine. On Windows it would be C:\Users\<<user_name>>\.gradle. Gradle then retrieves those dependencies during the project's building, testing, or packaging. Having a local cache reduces the load on the remote repositories and improves build speed.

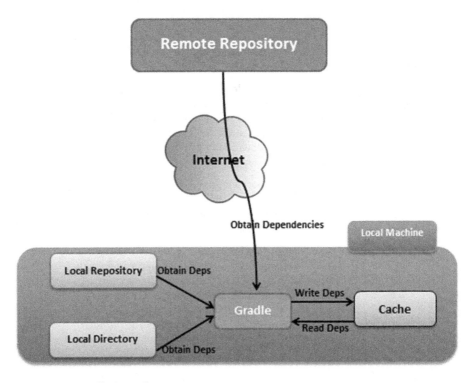

Figure 6-1. *Gradle dependency management*

■ **Tip**   You can change the default Gradle's home directory from `.gradle` by setting the
environment variable `GRADLE_USER_HOME` and pointing it to a new directory.

Although the architecture in Figure 6-1 works for small projects, it poses some
serious problems in an enterprise setting. Remote repositories accessed via the Internet
can go down or become unresponsive in high traffic situations, causing your builds to
slow down drastically. Licensing and intellectual property issues might prevent teams
from publishing their internal artifacts in public repositories, thereby preventing them
from being shared easily. To address those situations, most enterprises opt for the
architecture shown in Figure 6-2.

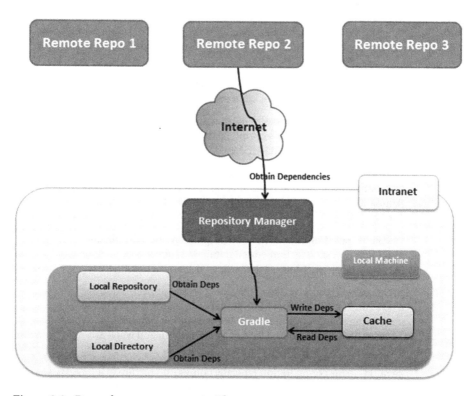

Figure 6-2. Dependency management with repo manager

The internal repository manager serves as a proxy to remote repositories and caches
artifacts. This ensures that builds are repeatable even if a remote repository were to be
down or became obsolete. The repository manager also allows you to push and share
your company's internal artifacts. Several open source and commercial repository
managers are available such as Sonatype Nexus, Apache Archiva, and Artifactory.

Dependency Configuration

Consider the earlier example of using Logback for logging. The source code will contain log statements that use Logback classes and API. For the project code to be compiled, you need the Logback JAR to be available in the classpath. Also, for the application to run inside a container such as Tomcat, you need the Logback JAR to be bundled inside the generated WAR artifact. Now consider the same project using JUnit for unit testing. The JUnit JAR file is needed only when you run unit tests and does need not be bundled in the generated WAR artifact. If the web application contains Java servlets, it would need the Servlet API JAR during code compilation. Since containers such as Tomcat make this API JAR available on classpath during runtime, you don't have to bundle it inside the WAR file.

These examples indicate the need to have certain sets of dependencies available at certain points of the build. Gradle has configurations that allow you to accomplish this easily. A *configuration* is a logical group of dependencies. For example, you can have a compile configuration that has all the dependencies needed during code compilation time. The Java plugin out-of-the-box declares the following six configurations:

- compile—Contains dependencies that are added to the classpath during code compilation. In a web project, dependencies such as Hibernate and Spring are declared in the compile configuration.

- runtime—Contains dependencies that are used during the execution of the code. For example, database drivers such as MySQL driver are declared in the runtime configuration.

- testCompile—Contains dependencies that become part of classpath during test code compilation. Test frameworks such as JUnit and TestNG are good examples of libraries declared in this configuration.

- testRuntime—Contains dependencies that are used during the execution of test code. Embedded databases such as HSQLDB or H2 are examples of libraries declared in this configuration.

- archives—Contains artifacts generated by the project. Consider a Java project that produces additional artifacts such as a JAR file containing source code and a ZIP file containing Javadoc API. These artifacts are declared in this configuration. You will learn more about archives configuration in Chapter 8.

- default—This configuration typically comes into picture in a multi-project setting where a project's build depends on another subproject's build. Consider the scenario where project A declares project B as its dependency. By default, all the artifacts in project B's default configuration will be included in project A. The default configuration extends the runtime configuration and hence contains all artifacts and dependencies declared in the project's runtime.

Dependency configurations can extend other configurations. The `runtime` configuration, for example, extends the `compile` configuration. What this means is that all the dependencies declared in the compile configuration will be available in the `runtime` configuration. Table 6-1 shows the six Java plugin configurations and the configurations they extend.

Table 6-1. *Configurations Inheritance*

Configuration Name	Extends From
compile	None
runtime	compile
testCompile	compile
testRuntime	runtime, testCompile
archives	None
default	runtime

Working with Dependencies

Before you can start declaring and using dependencies, it's important to understand the different types of dependencies. Table 6-2 shows the types provided by Gradle.

Table 6-2. *Gradle Dependency Types*

Dependency Type	Description
External module dependency	Dependency on a library in a repository. A dependency on the Logback JAR residing in Maven Central is an example this dependency type.
Project dependency	Dependency on a Gradle project.
File dependency	Dependency on files on the local machine.
Client module dependency	Dependency on an external module where the module is located in an external repository but the corresponding metadata is specified in a build file.
Gradle API dependency	Dependency on Gradle API. You saw this dependency type in Chapter 5 during plugin development.
Local Groovy dependency	Dependency on the Groovy libraries that came as part of the installed Gradle.

In this chapter, you look at using three dependency types—*external module, file,* and *project* dependencies. You declare dependencies in a build file using the dependencies closure as shown here:

```
dependencies {
    <dependency configuration> dependency1, dependency2....
}
```

External Module Dependencies

External module dependencies, as the name suggests, refer to dependencies on artifacts external to the current project structure. Dependencies of this type are specified using the following coordinates:

- group—Identifier of the group or organization responsible for this project. Examples include org.springframework and org.hibernate.

- name—The name of the artifact. Examples include spring-beans and hibernate-core.

- version—The version of the artifact. Examples include 1.0.0 and 4.2.0.

- classifier—Additional field attached to the artifact. For example, the same artifact can be released for 2 JDK versions and a classifier can be used to select the right one.

These dependencies can be declared using the following format in a build.gradle file:

```
group: 'GROUP_NAME, name: 'ARTIFACT_NAME', version: 'VERSION_NUMBER'
```

Gradle also provides the following shortcut format for declaring dependencies:

```
GROUP_NAME:ARTIFACT_NAME:VERSION_NUMBER
```

To see external module dependencies in action, create a new folder gradle_dep on your local machine. Create a build.gradle file and copy the contents from Listing 6-1. This example adds two dependencies for compile configuration using the shortcut notation. Notice that multiple dependencies are separated with a comma (,). It declares the two additional testCompile dependencies using the ArrayList notation. Also notice the repositories block. You will be learning about repositories later in this chapter, so for now you can ignore it.

Listing 6-1. The build.gradle File with Dependencies

```
apply plugin: 'java'

dependencies {
    compile 'ch.qos.logback:logback-classic:1.1.2', 'org.apache.
commons:commons-lang3:3.4'

    testCompile (
        [group: 'junit', name: 'junit', version: '4.12'],
        [group: 'org.hsqldb', name: 'hsqldb', version: '2.3.3']
    )
}
repositories {
    mavenCentral()
}
```

Gradle provides a built-in dependencies tasks that can be used to see the declared dependencies and their transitive dependencies. Running the command gradle dependencies will show output similar to this:

```
\chapter6\gradle-dep>gradle dependencies
................
compile - Compile classpath for source set 'main'.
Download https://repo1.maven.org/maven2/org/apache/commons/commons-
lang3/3.4/com
mons-lang3-3.4.pom
Download https://repo1.maven.org/maven2/org/apache/commons/commons-
parent/37/com
mons-parent-37.pom
Download https://repo1.maven.org/maven2/org/apache/apache/16/apache-16.pom
Download https://repo1.maven.org/maven2/org/slf4j/slf4j-api/1.7.6/slf4j-
api-1.7.
6.pom
Download https://repo1.maven.org/maven2/org/slf4j/slf4j-parent/1.7.6/slf4j-
paren
t-1.7.6.pom
+--- ch.qos.logback:logback-classic:1.1.2
|    +--- ch.qos.logback:logback-core:1.1.2
|    \--- org.slf4j:slf4j-api:1.7.6
\--- org.apache.commons:commons-lang3:3.4


..................

testCompile - Compile classpath for source set 'test'.
Download https://repo1.maven.org/maven2/org/hsqldb/hsqldb/2.3.3/hsqldb-
2.3.3.pom
```

```
+--- ch.qos.logback:logback-classic:1.1.2
|     +--- ch.qos.logback:logback-core:1.1.2
|     \--- org.slf4j:slf4j-api:1.7.6
+--- org.apache.commons:commons-lang3:3.4
+--- junit:junit:4.12
|     \--- org.hamcrest:hamcrest-core:1.3
\--- org.hsqldb:hsqldb:2.3.3
...............
```

From the output you will notice that all compile-time dependencies are available as runtime dependencies due to configuration inheritance. You are now ready to start using the Java classes/API provided by these libraries in your project.

In projects that contain a lot of dependencies, it is recommended to extract dependency versions into properties. This makes it easy to quickly identify artifact versions or change them during upgrades. Listing 6-2 shows modified build.gradle file with version numbers extracted to project level properties inside the ext closure. The dependency declarations are modified to use GStrings with version expressions. At runtime, these expressions will be replaced with the right version values.

Listing 6-2. The build.gradle File with Properties

```
apply plugin: 'java'

ext {
    logbackVersion = '1.1.2'
    commonsLangVersion = '3.4'
    junitVersion = '4.12'
    hsqlDbVersion = '2.3.3'
}

dependencies {
    compile "ch.qos.logback:logback-classic:$logbackVersion", "org.apache.
    commons:commons-lang3:$commonsLangVersion"

    testCompile (
                    [group: 'junit', name: 'junit', version:
                    "$junitVersion"],
                    [group: 'org.hsqldb', name: 'hsqldb', version:
                    "$hsqlDbVersion"]
    )
}

repositories {
        mavenCentral()
}
```

In projects containing a lot of dependencies, you run into another common problem where you end up repeating the same group and version numbers in multiple places. For example, consider a Java project using the 3.0 version of Spring Framework libraries such as spring-core, spring-aop, spring-beans, spring-jdbc, and spring-context. Listing 6-3 shows the build-common-group.gradle file demonstrating an approach to address this duplication issue. The artifact names are grouped into a list. The code iterates through the list, registering each dependency as a compile-time configuration. You can run the build script using the command gradle -b build-common-group.gradle dependencies.

Listing 6-3. The build-common-group.gradle File

```
apply plugin: 'java'

ext { springVersion = '3.0.0.RELEASE' }

dependencies {

        ['spring-core', 'spring-aop','spring-beans', 'spring-jdbc', 'spring-
        context'].each {
                compile "org.springframework:$it:$springVersion"
        }
}
repositories {
      mavenCentral()
}
```

File Dependencies

Most legacy projects contain dependencies inside a lib folder in their project or in a folder on a shared drive. Gradle's file dependency type allows you to use such files directly in your project. This type is especially useful during legacy project migrations or when you don't have a private repository to host internal libraries.

To better understand file dependency type, let's create a new project named gradle-file-dep. Create the gradle-file-dep folder on your file system and an empty build.gradle file. Inside this folder, create a lib subfolder and populate it with a couple of JAR files. Table 6-3 lists the JAR files you will be using along with the links to download them from the Internet.

Table 6-3. *JAR Files Inside the lib Folder*

JAR File	Download URL
logback-classic-1.1.3.jar	http://search.maven.org/ remotecontent?filepath=ch/qos/logback/ logback-classic/1.1.3/logback-classic- 1.1.3.jar
commons-lang3-3.4.jar	http://search.maven.org/ remotecontent?filepath=org/apache/commons/ commons-lang3/3.4/commons-lang3-3.4.jar
spring-core-4.2.3.RELEASE.jar	http://search.maven.org/ remotecontent?filepath=org/ springframework/spring-core/4.2.3.RELEASE/ spring-core-4.2.3.RELEASE.jar
slf4j-api-1.7.13.jar	http://search.maven.org/ remotecontent?filepath=org/slf4j/slf4j- api/1.7.13/slf4j-api-1.7.13.jar

At this point, the project should have the directory structure shown in Figure 6-3.

```
─gradle-file-dep
 │    build.gradle
 │
 └──lib
         commons-lang3-3.4.jar
         logback-classic-1.1.3.jar
         slf4j-api-1.7.13.jar
         spring-core-4.2.3.RELEASE.jar
```

Figure 6-3. *The gradle-file-dep folder structure*

Adding files as dependencies to your project involves passing in a file collection to Gradle. As the name suggests, a file collection is simply a set of files. The easiest way to work with a file collection is to use the Project.files() method. This method takes a variable number of objects as parameters and attempts to convert them into sets of java. io.File instances. Listing 6-4 shows the build.gradle file with two file dependencies added to the compile configuration.

Listing 6-4. The build.gradle with two File Dependencies

```
apply plugin: 'java'
dependencies {
    compile files ("lib/logback-classic-1.1.3.jar", "lib/commons-lang3-3.4.jar")
}
```

Instead of spelling out each file as a dependency, there are occasions where you might want to include all or a subset of files in a folder. You can accomplish that using project's fileTree method. A file tree represents a hierarchy of files, such as directory. Listing 6-5 shows the updated build.gradle file that adds all the JAR files inside the lib directory to the compile configuration.

Listing 6-5. File Dependency Type Using File Trees

```
apply plugin: 'java'
dependencies {
    compile fileTree (dir : "lib", include: "*.jar")
}
```

File dependencies are not included in the project's dependency descriptor. Hence, running the command gradle dependencies will not list the file dependency JARs on the console. To see those JARs, append the displayJars task shown in Listing 6-6 to the build.gradle file. The task uses the collect() method to iterate through all the dependencies in the compile configuration and prints their names.

Listing 6-6. The displayJars Task

```
task displayJars << {
    println "${configurations.compile.collect {File f -> f.name}}"
}
```

Using a command prompt, run the gradle -q displayJars command inside the project folder. You should see the following output:

```
\gradle-file-dep>gradle -q displayJars
[commons-lang3-3.4.jar, logback-classic-1.1.3.jar, slf4j-api-1.7.13.jar,
spring-
core-4.2.3.RELEASE.jar]
```

Project Dependencies

Complex enterprise projects are often split into smaller projects. For example, an online application might be broken into three separate projects—a web project containing UI related assets and components, a services project that contains backend services, and a repository project that contains repository/DAO code to access a database backend. In such scenarios, the web project depends on the service project, which in turn depends on the repository project. Gradle provides the project dependency type to establish such dependencies.

Project dependencies can be declared using the project's project() method, which takes the name of the dependent project. Listing 6-7 shows an example of a "web" project depending on the service project. The colon (:) character denotes project hierarchy. Hence the string ":service" indicates that the service project is one level underneath the root.

Listing 6-7. The Project Dependency Type

```
dependencies {
    compile project (":service")
}
```

With this project dependency, Gradle will include the generated `service.jar` artifact as a dependency in the web project. Additionally the service project's dependencies and their transitive dependencies are added as web project's dependencies. You will look at project dependencies in more detail and with examples in Chapter 7.

Resolving Dependency Conflicts

Consider a Gradle project named `transitive-dep` that uses the Spring Core library (`spring-core.jar`) and Apache HttpClient (`httpclient.jar`). Listing 6-8 shows the project's `build.gradle` file with the two compile-time dependencies.

Listing 6-8. Version Conflict Example

```
apply plugin: 'java'

dependencies {
    compile 'org.springframework:spring-core:4.2.2.RELEASE',
    'org.apache.httpcomponents:httpclient:4.0'
}
repositories {
    mavenCentral()
}
```

Both the Spring Core and HttpClient libraries use Apache Commons Logging as their underlying logging framework. However, the version 4.2.2 of Spring Core uses Commons Logging version 1.2, while version 4.0 of HttpClient uses Commons Logging version 1.1. When such version conflicts arise, Gradle by default uses the latest version of the transitive dependency. Output of the `gradle dependencies` command shows this resolution strategy:

```
\chapter6\transitive-dep>gradle dependencies
    ----------
compile - Compile classpath for source set 'main'.
+--- org.springframework:spring-core:4.2.2.RELEASE
|    \--- commons-logging:commons-logging:1.2
\--- org.apache.httpcomponents:httpclient:4.0
     +--- org.apache.httpcomponents:httpcore:4.0.1
     +--- commons-logging:commons-logging:1.1.1 -> 1.2
     \--- commons-codec:commons-codec:1.3
```

On occasions, you might not want Gradle to pick the latest JAR file. In such scenarios, you can change the default resolution strategy and force Gradle to include a certain version. Listing 6-9 shows the modified build.gradle file accomplishing this. The configurations{} block allows you to configure project's dependency configuration behavior. You then apply a resolutionStrategy block to all configurations. Finally, you use the force method to force the usage of 1.1.1 version of commons-logging dependency.

Listing 6-9. Resolution Strategy Forcing a Dependency

```
apply plugin: 'java'

configurations.all {
    resolutionStrategy {
        force 'commons-logging:commons-logging:1.1.1'
    }
}

dependencies {
    compile 'org.springframework:spring-core:4.2.2.RELEASE',
    'org.apache.httpcomponents:httpclient:4.0'
}
repositories {
    mavenCentral()
}
```

Running the gradle dependencies command on the modified build.gradle shows that the 1.1.1 version is being picked up over the 1.2 version:

```
default - Configuration for default artifacts.
+--- org.springframework:spring-core:4.2.2.RELEASE
|    \--- commons-logging:commons-logging:1.2 -> 1.1.1
\--- org.apache.httpcomponents:httpclient:4.0
     +--- org.apache.httpcomponents:httpcore:4.0.1
     +--- commons-logging:commons-logging:1.1.1
     \--- commons-codec:commons-codec:1.3
```

Though transitive dependencies are useful, they can cause problems and unpredictable side effects as you might end up with wrong versions of JARs in the project. To be proactive and troubleshoot issues when version conflicts arise, you can make Gradle fail the builds when version conflicts are found. You can change the default resolution strategy to fail on version conflicts using the failOnVersionConflict method. Listing 6-10 shows the modified build.gradle file using the failOnVersionConflict() method.

Listing 6-10. Resolution Strategy Failing on Conflicts

```
apply plugin: 'java'

configurations.all {
    resolutionStrategy {
        failOnVersionConflict()
    }
}

dependencies {
    compile 'org.springframework:spring-core:4.2.2.RELEASE',
    'org.apache.httpcomponents:httpclient:4.0'
}
repositories {
    mavenCentral()
}
```

From a command line, run the gradle dependencies command and you will see a failed report:

```
FAILURE: Build failed with an exception.

* What went wrong:
Execution failed for task ':dependencies'.
> Could not resolve all dependencies for configuration ':compile'.
    > A conflict was found between the following modules:
        - commons-logging:commons-logging:1.2
        - commons-logging:commons-logging:1.1.1
```

Repositories

As discussed at the beginning of this chapter, repositories contain dependencies and associated metadata. Gradle out-of-the-box can work with Maven, Ivy, and local directory repositories. It also provides a few preconfigured repositories that make it easy to interact with commonly used repositories. The mavenCentral() repository is one such preconfigured repository that points to Maven's central repository at https://repo1.maven.org/maven2. Listing 6-11 shows the configuration needed to interact with Maven Central. The repositories block is used to configure repositories used in a project.

Listing 6-11. Mavan Central Repository Config

```
repositories {
    mavenCentral()
}
```

JCenter is another popular repository that hosts artifacts at `https://bintray.com/bintray/jcenter`. Listing 6-12 shows the configuration to interact with JCenter repo.

Listing 6-12. JCenter Repository Config

```
repositories {
    jcenter()
}
```

More often than not, your company might have an internal Maven repository. Gradle provides a `maven()` method that makes it easy to add and configure a Maven repository. Listing 6-13 shows a custom Maven repository declaration. For repositories that need authentication, the configuration allows you to provide credentials.

Listing 6-13. Custom Maven Repository

```
apply plugin: 'java'

repositories {
    maven {
        url "http://your_repo.url"

        credentials {
            username 'user_name'
            password 'pwd'
        }
    }
}
```

In certain limited cases you might need to use a local Maven repository to retrieve dependencies. Local Maven repositories are typically located in the `USER_HOME/.m2` directory. For those scenarios, Gradle provides another preconfigured repository named `mavenLocal()`, as shown in Listing 6-14.

Listing 6-14. Maven Local Repository

```
apply plugin: 'java'

repositories {
    mavenLocal()
}
```

In cases where you are dealing with legacy projects, you might want to interact with libraries located in a local directory. Gradle supports such interactions with a flat directory repository. This shouldn't be confused with a Maven local repository. Maven local repositories contain artifacts and the associated metadata, such as a `pom.xml` file. However, a flat directory just contains JAR files and no metadata. Listing 6-15 shows the configuration to use JAR files from the `lib` folder.

Listing 6-15. Flat Directory Repository

```
apply plugin: 'java'

repositories {
    flatDir {
        dirs 'lib'
    }
}

dependencies {
        compile name: 'commons-lang3', version : '3.4'
       compile name: 'logback-classic', version: '1.1.3'
}
```

When working with flat directory repositories, you need to declare dependencies using the artifact's name and version attributes. Listing 6-15 declares the commons-lang3 library with the name and version attributes. During the build, Gradle will look for a JAR file with the name commons-lang3-3.4.jar inside the lib directory. If the logback-classic library is declared using just the name attribute, Gradle will look for a JAR named logback-classic.jar inside the lib folder.

Unlike file dependencies discussed in an earlier section, dependencies from flat directory repositories are included in the project's dependency descriptor. To verify this configuration, create a build-file-repository.gradle file inside the gradle-file-dep project and copy the contents of Listing 6-15. Run the gradle -b build-file-repository.gradle dependencies command in the project and it will list the following dependencies:

```
compile - Compile classpath for source set 'main'.
+--- :commons-lang3:3.4
\--- :logback-classic:1.1.3
```

Uber JAR Creation

For Java projects, Gradle generates a JAR file that contains compiled classes and other resources residing in the src/main/resources folder. However, there are scenarios when you'll want to distribute your Java application as a self-contained application that includes all its dependent JARs. A common technique to deliver such a bundle is to create an "uber" or "fat" JAR. In this section, you will generate an uber JAR of the gradle-dep project you have built in this chapter.

To build an uber JAR, you will use an open source plugin named Shadow. The plugin's page on the Gradle plugin portal at https://plugins.gradle.org/plugin/com.github.johnrengelman.shadow provides a script snippet (shown in Listing 6-16) to use the plugin.

Listing 6-16. Shadow Plugin Snippet

```
buildscript {
  repositories {
    maven {
      url "https://plugins.gradle.org/m2/"
    }
  }
  dependencies {
    classpath "com.github.jengelman.gradle.plugins:shadow:1.2.2"
  }
}

apply plugin: "com.github.johnrengelman.shadow"
```

The `buildscript` block in Listing 6-16 allows you to use third-party plugins such as Shadow. Inside the block, you declare the Gradle Plugin Maven repository located at `https://plugins.gradle.org/m2/`. This is followed by a `dependencies` block, where you add the plugin JAR to the build script's classpath.

Append the snippet in Listing 6-16 to the bottom of gradle-dep's `build.gradle` file. Listing 6-17 shows the complete `build.gradle` file you will be using.

Listing 6-17. The Build Script with Shadow Plugin

```
apply plugin: 'java'

ext {
    logbackVersion = '1.1.2'
    commonsLangVersion = '3.4'
    junitVersion = '4.12'
    hsqlDbVersion = '2.3.3'
}

dependencies {
    compile "ch.qos.logback:logback-classic:$logbackVersion",
    "org.apache.commons:commons-lang3:$commonsLangVersion"

    testCompile (
        [group: 'junit', name: 'junit', version: "$junitVersion"],
                            [group: 'org.hsqldb', name: 'hsqldb',
                                   version: "$hsqlDbVersion"]
    )
}

repositories {
    mavenCentral()
}
```

```
buildscript {
    repositories {
        maven {
            url "https://plugins.gradle.org/m2/"
        }
    }
    dependencies {
        classpath "com.github.jengelman.gradle.plugins:shadow:1.2.2"
    }
}

apply plugin: "com.github.johnrengelman.shadow"
```

Run the gradle shadowJar command inside the gradle-dep project and you should see this output:

```
\chapter6\gradle-dep>gradle shadowJar
:compileJava UP-TO-DATE
:processResources UP-TO-DATE
:classes UP-TO-DATE
:shadowJar

BUILD SUCCESSFUL
```

Upon successful completion of the task, navigate to the build/libs folder under the project and you should see a gradle-dep-all.jar. The JAR file should contain classes from the Logback and Apache Commons Lang, as shown in Figure 6-4.

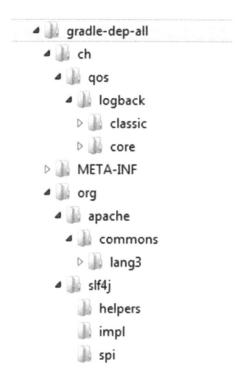

Figure 6-4. *Extracted directory structure of gradle-dep-all*

Summary

Projects typically depend on internal or third-party libraries. Gradle provides excellent support for declaring and managing these dependencies. This chapter reviewed the basics of declarative dependencies, and you learned how to group dependencies using dependency configurations. You also learned about three dependency types—external module, file, and project. External module dependencies are declared using group, name, and version attributes, while file dependencies are declared using their names. The chapter then reviewed how Gradle resolves dependency conflicts and how to configure the resolution strategies. Finally, you learned about the role repositories play in dependency management and the several repository types that Gradle supports.

The next chapter covers Gradle's support for multi-projects.

CHAPTER 7

■ ■ ■

Multi-Project Builds

Complex enterprise projects are often split into several subprojects to ease development, maintainability, and increase reuse. This chapter reviews how multi-projects are structured and configured. You will build a sample multi-project to better understand Gradle's multi-project support. You will look at approaches for distributing build logic across root and subprojects. You will also learn how to execute single project builds or a full project build and declare dependencies between projects.

Multi-Project Structure

Gradle supports development of complex projects by allowing multiple Gradle projects to be nested under a single root Gradle project. The root project allows you to define common dependencies and build logic instead of spreading it across individual projects. Instead of building each subproject individually, the root project provides one place to perform a full build of all projects. The layout of a hierarchically structured multi-project is shown in Figure 7-1.

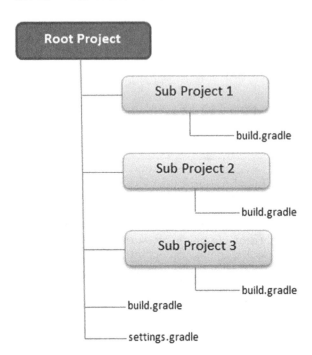

Figure 7-1. *Standard hierarchical multi-project layout*

The root project contains three subproject folders, a build.gradle file, and a settings.gradle file. Each subproject can contain an optional build.gradle file. To better understand the multi-project builds and the significance of the settings.gradle file, you will see how to implement a sample multi-project in the next section.

Sample Project

This sample multi-project is made up of a web subproject that contains a user interface (WAR artifact), a service project (JAR artifact) that contains a service layer code, and a repository project (JAR artifact) that contains a persistence layer and entity code. The UI layer code relies on the service layer code to complete the web requests. Hence, the web subproject has a dependency over the service subproject. The service layer code delegates all persistence operations to the repository layer. Hence, the service subproject has a dependency over the repository subproject. Figure 7-2 provides a visual representation of this dependency scenario.

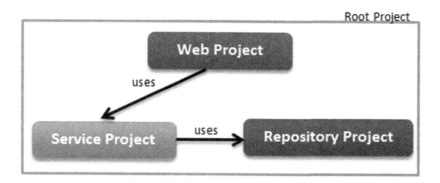

Figure 7-2. *Sample project dependencies*

Begin the sample multi-project implementation by creating the following folder structure on your local machine.

```
intro-root
    web
    service
    repository
```

The root project is intro-root and the subprojects are web, service, and repository. Create an empty build.gradle file in the root project and run the gradle projects command. The task projects is a built-in Gradle task that displays subprojects in a hierarchical fashion. The output of the command is as follows:

```
\chapter7\intro-root>gradle projects
:projects

------------------------------------------------------------
Root project
------------------------------------------------------------

Root project 'intro-root'
No sub-projects

To see a list of the tasks of a project, run gradle <project-path>:tasks
For example, try running gradle :tasks

BUILD SUCCESSFUL
```

From the output you can see that Gradle found the root project `intro-root` but didn't find any subprojects inside it. This is where the `settings.gradle` comes into picture. In this file, you specify the subprojects that Gradle needs to include in the build. Let's fix the build by creating a `settings.gradle` file inside the `intro-root` folder. You then use the `include` method to add the three subprojects, as shown. The `include` method takes the subproject directory names as its parameters.

```
include 'web', 'service', 'repository'
```

Upon running the `gradle projects` command, you will see that Gradle detects all four projects (including root):

```
\chapter7\intro-root>gradle projects
:projects

------------------------------------------------------------
Root project
------------------------------------------------------------

Root project 'intro-root'
+--- Project ':repository'
+--- Project ':service'
\--- Project ':web'

To see a list of the tasks of a project, run gradle <project-path>:tasks
For example, try running gradle :repository:tasks

BUILD SUCCESSFUL
```

The output also shows Gradle's use of ":" to indicate project hierarchy. For example, `:service` indicates that the service project is one level below the root (referred implicitly without a name). If your project exists under `service/soap/util`, then it will be referred to using `:service:soap:util`.

Flat Layout

In addition to the hierarchical project layout you saw in the previous section, Gradle supports a "flat layout" for multi-project development. In this organization, all the projects exist as siblings of the root project. Figure 7-3 shows the `intro-root` multi-project organized using the flat layout.

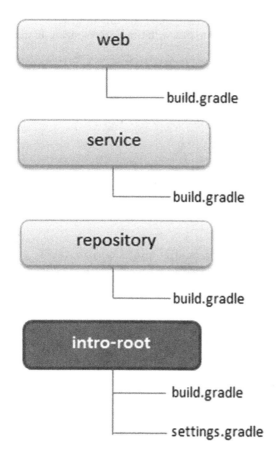

Figure 7-3. *intro-root in flat layout*

To get familiar with the flat layout way of organizing projects, recreate the intro-root sample application. Start by creating a folder named flat-layout on your local file system. Inside this folder, create four subfolders—web, service, repository, and intro-root. Under intro-root, create an empty build.gradle file and an empty settings.gradle file. With flat layouts, you use the includeFlat method instead of the include method for including projects. The includeFlat method takes the directory names of the subprojects as its parameters. Copy these contents into settings.gradle file:

```
includeFlat 'web', 'service', 'repository'
```

Using command prompt, navigate to the `intro-root` folder and run the gradle `projects` command. You should see output similar to this, with Gradle recognizing all the projects:

```
\chapter7\flat-layout\intro-root>gradle projects
:projects

------------------------------------------------------------
Root project
------------------------------------------------------------

Root project 'intro-root'
+--- Project ':repository'
+--- Project ':service'
\--- Project ':web'

To see a list of the tasks of a project, run gradle <project-path>:tasks
For example, try running gradle :repository:tasks

BUILD SUCCESSFUL
```

The choice of a hierarchical or flat layout for organizing your project is purely your personal preference. We find the hierarchical layout much cleaner and the "hierarchical" `intro-root` project is used in this chapter.

Multi-Project vs. Single-Project Builds

The root project's `build.gradle` file can be used to trigger a full build of all projects. However, it is possible for the subprojects to contain an optional `build.gradle` file. Gradle allows you to execute stand-alone builds on any of these subprojects. In that scenario, only the subproject and any dependent projects are built.

So how would Gradle know if a build is a single-project build or part of a larger multi-project build? To make this determination, Gradle looks for the `settings.gradle` file using the following algorithm:

1. Look for the `settings.gradle` in the current directory.

2. If `settings.gradle` is not found, look for it under a `master` directory that is at the same level of nesting as the current directory.

3. If `settings.gradle` is not found, look for it under any parent directories.

Upon finding a `settings.gradle` file, a check is made to determine if the current project is defined as part of a multi-project using the `include` or `includeFlat` methods. If the condition is met, the build is executed as a multi-project build. Otherwise, the project is executed as a single-project build.

Project Configuration

The subprojects in a multi-project often contain common configuration, tasks, and plugins that can be moved to the root project's build.gradle file. For example, all projects would share the same group and version number attributes. Gradle provides an allprojects closure block that allows you to define such common attributes/behavior shared by root project as well as subprojects. Listing 7-1 shows an allprojects block with group and version attributes declared.

Listing 7-1. The allprojects Block in build.grade

```
allprojects {
    group = "com.apress.gradle"
    version = "1.0.0-SNAPSHOT"
}
```

Similarly, if all subprojects are Java projects, they would all have the java plugin applied to them. They would also share common repositories and possibly share few dependencies as well. To define such behavior specific to all subprojects, Gradle provides a subprojects closure block. Listing 7-2 shows a subprojects block containing the java plugin and the mavenCentral() repository declaration.

Listing 7-2. The subprojects Closure Block in build.gradle

```
subprojects {
    apply plugin: 'java'

    repositories {
        mavenCentral()
    }
}
```

■ **Note**   The allprojects block should be used to declare attributes/configuration/tasks that apply to all projects. IDE plugins are good examples of plugins that can be declared inside the allprojects section.

It is also possible to configure behavior specific to a single subproject in the root project's build.gradle file. For example, you need to apply the war plugin to the web project. You can add this project-specific behavior using the project() method and then pass in the project name you want to configure as its parameter. Listing 7-3 shows the configuration to apply a war plugin to the web project.

Listing 7-3. Project-Specific Behavior

```
project(':web') {
    apply plugin: 'war'
}
```

You apply the concepts discussed so far in this section to create an intro-root's build.gradle file shown in Listing 7-4. It uses the allprojects block to ensure that root and subprojects share the same group and version numbers. The code also uses the subprojects block to ensure that all the subprojects get their dependencies from Maven Central. The individual project blocks apply the java plugin to the service and repository projects and apply the war plugin to the web project.

Listing 7-4. The Intro-Project's build.gradle File

```
allprojects {
    group = "com.apress.gradle"
    version = "1.0.0-SNAPSHOT"
}

subprojects {
    repositories {
        mavenCentral()
    }
}

project (':service') {
    apply plugin: 'java'
}

project (':repository') {
    apply plugin: 'java'
}

project(':web') {
    apply plugin: 'war'
}
```

With the intro-root project's build.gradle file updated, run the gradle build command and you will see this output:

```
\chapter7\intro-root>gradle build
:repository:compileJava UP-TO-DATE
:repository:processResources UP-TO-DATE
:repository:classes UP-TO-DATE
:repository:jar
```

```
........................
:repository:build
:service:compileJava UP-TO-DATE
:service:processResources UP-TO-DATE
:service:classes UP-TO-DATE
:service:jar
:service:assemble
........................
:web:compileJava UP-TO-DATE
:web:processResources UP-TO-DATE
:web:classes UP-TO-DATE
:web:war
:web:assemble
........................
:web:build

BUILD SUCCESSFUL
```

From the output, notice that Gradle by default executes the subprojects in ascending order of their alphanumeric names.

Project Dependencies

As you saw in Figure 7-2, the web project depends on the service project and the service project has dependency on the repository project. Gradle provides the project dependency type to declare such dependencies. Listing 7-5 shows the modified build. gradle section declaring these two dependencies.

Listing 7-5. Project Dependencies in build.gradle

```
allprojects {
    group = "com.apress.gradle"
    version = "1.0.0-SNAPSHOT"
}

subprojects {
    repositories {
        mavenCentral()
    }
}

project (':repository') {
    apply plugin: 'java'
}
```

```
project (':service') {
    apply plugin: 'java'
    dependencies {
        compile project(':repository')
    }
}

project(':web') {
    apply plugin: 'war'
    dependencies {
        compile project(':service')
    }
}
```

If you were to execute gradle build now, Gradle will attempt to build the repository project, followed by the service and then the web project. The output should resemble Gradle's default output. However, if you were to tweak the dependencies such that web depends on repository and the repository depends on the service, running gradle build would assemble the service JAR before running the repository build:

```
\chapter7\intro-root>gradle build
:service:compileJava UP-TO-DATE
:service:processResources UP-TO-DATE
:service:classes UP-TO-DATE
:service:jar UP-TO-DATE
:repository:compileJava UP-TO-DATE
............................
:repository:check UP-TO-DATE
:repository:build UP-TO-DATE
:service:assemble UP-TO-DATE
............................
:web:compileTestJava UP-TO-DATE
:web:processTestResources UP-TO-DATE
:web:testClasses UP-TO-DATE
:web:test UP-TO-DATE
:web:check UP-TO-DATE
:web:build

BUILD SUCCESSFUL
```

Subproject Build Files

So far you have been using the root project's build.gradle file to declare common as well as project-specific behavior, thereby eliminating the need for individual build.gradle files in each subproject. For large projects, this technique would result in a complex single build.gradle file. For ease of maintenance, you might want to limit the root project's build.gradle file to contain only the common behavior and split the rest of the configuration into individual subproject build files.

To see this in action, create a build.gradle file under the service project and copy the contents shown in Listing 7-6. From the root project's build.gradle file, remove the project(':service'){} block.

Listing 7-6. The Service Project Specific Configuration

```
apply plugin: 'java'

dependencies {
    compile project(':repository')
}
```

Using a command prompt, navigate to the service folder and run the gradle build command. You will see that this triggers a repository JAR build followed by the service project's build:

```
\chapter7\intro-root\service>gradle build
:repository:compileJava UP-TO-DATE
:repository:processResources UP-TO-DATE
:repository:classes UP-TO-DATE
:repository:jar UP-TO-DATE
:service:compileJava UP-TO-DATE
:service:processResources UP-TO-DATE
:service:classes UP-TO-DATE
:service:jar UP-TO-DATE
:service:assemble UP-TO-DATE
:service:compileTestJava UP-TO-DATE
:service:processTestResources UP-TO-DATE
:service:testClasses UP-TO-DATE
:service:test UP-TO-DATE
:service:check UP-TO-DATE
:service:build UP-TO-DATE

BUILD SUCCESSFUL
```

Summary

In this chapter, you learned about the intricacies of Gradle's multi-project builds. You looked at the two types of project structure—hierarchical and flat. You learned about allprojects, subprojects, and project blocks, which allow you to place build logic in the right locations to improve maintainability. You then learned how to declare dependencies across your projects. Finally, you reviewed how to trigger a full build and a subproject build.

In the next chapter, you learn about Gradle's support for publishing generated artifacts to repositories.

CHAPTER 8

■ ■ ■

Publishing Artifacts

In order to share internally developed frameworks and libraries, developers need to publish them to repositories. In this chapter, you will use Gradle to publish artifacts to local file system and an repository.

Publishing to a Local Repository

The projects you work with typically generate one or more artifacts such as JAR, WAR, or ZIP files. Gradle provides an archives configuration that can be used to declare the artifacts produced by a project. A Java project by default produces a JAR file and hence the Java plugin automatically associates the generated JAR to the archives configuration. Similarly, the War plugin assigns the generated WAR to this configuration. Gradle provides an uploadArchives task that can be used to publish these artifacts to repositories.

To better understand the publishing process, you'll create an empty Java application named sample-app. To do this, create a new folder called sample-app on your file system. Then create a build.gradle file and copy the contents of Listing 8-1.

Listing 8-1. sample-app build.gradle file

```
apply plugin: 'java'
version = 1.0

uploadArchives {
    repositories {
      flatDir { dirs "../repo" }
    }
}
```

The repositories closure in the uploadArchives task allows you to configure the location where the artifacts should be published. Listing 8-1 is asking Gradle to publish the generated artifact to a repo folder located at the same level as sample-app folder on the file system. To perform the publishing, run the following uploadArchives task:

```
\chapter8\sample-app>gradle uploadArchives
```

Upon successful execution, you will see a repo folder created with contents, as shown in Figure 8-1.

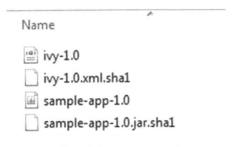

Name

📄 ivy-1.0
📄 ivy-1.0.xml.sha1
📄 sample-app-1.0
📄 sample-app-1.0.jar.sha1

Figure 8-1. *The repo folder's contents*

Gradle by default uses the projectname-version.type format for the generated file names. Hence, the generated artifact is named sample-app-1.0.jar. Additionally, Gradle generates an ivy.xml configuration file and adds it to the repo folder.

This published artifact is now ready to be accessed in other projects. As discussed in Chapter 6, a straightforward approach is to declare this folder as a "flat directory repository" and add sample-app as a dependency.

Publishing to a Maven Repository

In order to publish to a Maven repository, you need a pom.xml configuration file along with the artifact. The Project Object Model or pom.xml file describes the artifact and contains information such as dependencies and plugins. Gradle provides a Maven plugin that simplifies deployments to Maven repositories and can automatically generate the pom.xml file.

Before you can start publishing to a Maven repository, you need access to a repository manager such as Artifactory (www.jfrog.com/artifactory/) or Nexus (www.sonatype.org/nexus/go/). Repository managers manage repositories, act as proxies of public repositories, and enable governance of artifacts used in the enterprise. In the next section, you will look at installing Nexus, which is a popular open source repository manager from Sonatype, on your local machine.

Installing Nexus

Nexus is distributed as an archive, and it comes bundled with a Jetty instance. Download the Nexus distribution (.zip version for Windows) from Sonatype's web site at www.sonatype.org/nexus/go/. At the time of this writing, version 2.11.4-01 of Nexus is available. Unzip the file and place the contents on your machine. The code in this book assumes the contents to be in the C:\tools\nexus folder.

Launch your command line in administrator mode and navigate to the `bin` folder located in `C:\tools\nexus\nexus-2.11.4-01`. To start Nexus, run the following command:

```
nexus console
```

By default, Nexus runs on port 8081. Launch a web browser and navigate to Nexus at `http://localhost:8081/nexus`. Figure 8-2 shows the Nexus launch screen. Sign in to the application using the Log In link in the top-right corner. The default login username and password for Nexus are `admin` and `admin123`.

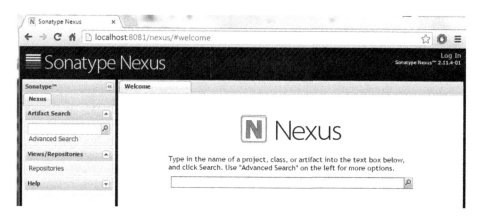

Figure 8-2. *Nexus index page*

The Build Configuration

Now that you have Nexus repository manager running, the next step is to modify the `build.gradle` file. Listing 8-2 shows the updated `build.gradle` file with configuration needed to publish to a Maven repository.

Listing 8-2. build.gradle for Publishing to Maven Repo

```
apply plugin: 'java'
apply plugin: 'maven'

group = 'com.apress.gradle.intro'
archivesBaseName = 'sample-app'
version = '1.0-SNAPSHOT'

uploadArchives {
    repositories {
        mavenDeployer {
            repository (url: "http://localhost:8081/nexus/content/
            repositories/releases") {
```

```
                authentication (userName: "deployment", password: "deployment123")
                }
                snapshotRepository (url: "http://localhost:8081/nexus/content/
                repositories/snapshots") {
                authentication (userName: "deployment", password: "deployment123")
                }
            }
        }
}

dependencies {
    compile 'ch.qos.logback:logback-classic:1.1.2'
}
repositories {
    mavenCentral()
}
```

For Gradle to generate the pom.xml file, it needs three Maven coordinates—groupId, artifactId, and version. In Listing 8-2, you use Project's group, archivesBaseName, and version properties to provide those values. Gradle provides the mavenDeployer method, which allows you to configure the Maven repositories to publish artifacts. In Listing 8-2, you configured a snapshotRepository (http://localhost:8081/nexus/content/ repositories/snapshots) to publish SNAPSHOT or development versions of artifacts and a release repository (http://localhost:8081/nexus/content/repositories/releases) for released artifacts. For Gradle to publish artifacts to Nexus, it needs to provide appropriate credentials. In the build script, you are using the deployment user (password: deployment 123) that comes by default with Nexus installation. The deployment user has the "Nexus Deployment Role" with privileges to write to repositories. This code then adds a logback dependency to the project followed by a repositories block pointing to Maven Central. The mavenCentral() configuration tells Gradle to download the logback dependency from Maven Central. Although this configuration could have used Nexus for downloading dependencies, it provides the possibility of using separate repositories for downloading and uploading artifacts.

With this configuration in place, run the gradle uploadArchives command and you will see this output:

```
\chapter8\sample-app>gradle uploadArchives
:compileJava UP-TO-DATE
:processResources UP-TO-DATE
:classes UP-TO-DATE
:jar
:uploadArchives
```

```
Could not find metadata com.apress.gradle.intro:sample-app:1.0-SNAPSHOT/
maven-metadata.xml in remote (http://localhost:8081/nexus/content/
repositories/snapshots)
Could not find metadata com.apress.gradle.intro:sample-app/maven-metadata.
xml in remote (http://localhost:8081/nexus/content/repositories/snapshots)
```

BUILD SUCCESSFUL

The "Could not find metadata ..." error in this output is simply a warning indicating that Gradle wasn't able to find a metadata.xml file for this artifact on the Nexus server. You would see this message when an artifact is being published for the first time. The metadata.xml file would get created on first publish and hence you should not see this message in future publishes.

Using your browser, navigate to the Nexus Console at http://localhost:8081/nexus/. From the vertical navigation on the left, click the Repositories link. You will see all user-managed repositories displayed in the right pane. Since you published a SNAPSHOT version of the artifact, click the repository path link next to Snapshots (http://localhost:8081/nexus/content/repositories/snapshots/). This will launch the Snapshot repository in a new browser tab. Click through the links com->apress->gradle->intro->sample-app->1.0-SNAPSHOT and you will see the generated artifacts, as shown in Figure 8-3.

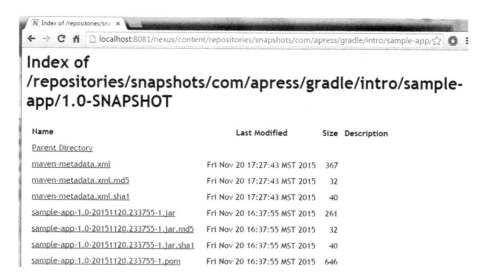

Figure 8-3. *Sample app artifacts on Nexus*

You can also use the URL http://localhost:8081/nexus/content/repositories/ snapshots/com/apress/gradle/intro/sample-app/1.0-SNAPSHOT/ to directly access the generated artifacts. Notice that Nexus uses the artifact's group name (com.apress.gradle.intro), artifact's name (sample-app), and artifact's version (1.0-SNAPSHOT) to construct this URL.

Open the generated sample-app-1.0-#########.pom file and you will see that Gradle has automatically added project's logback dependency as a Maven dependency:

```
<project ".....">
        <modelVersion>4.0.0</modelVersion>
        <groupId>com.apress.gradle.intro</groupId>
        <artifactId>sample-app</artifactId>
        <version>1.0-SNAPSHOT</version>

        <dependencies>
            <dependency>
                <groupId>ch.qos.logback</groupId>
                <artifactId>logback-classic</artifactId>
                <version>1.1.2</version>
                <scope>compile</scope>
            </dependency>
        </dependencies>
</project>
```

Dealing with Additional Artifacts

Earlier in the chapter you learned that the archives configuration is used to declare artifacts produced by a project. Plugins such as Java automatically associate the generated JAR file with this configuration. However, if your project produces additional artifacts (for example, a source JAR or a Javadoc JAR), you need to explicitly associate those with the archives configuration in your build file. You achieve this by providing to the archives configuration, the actual artifact or a task that produces the artifact.

To better understand this concept, consider the scenario where you want sample-app to distribute the following artifacts:

- A properties file named app.properties located at the root of the project.

- A JAR file containing the project's source code

To follow along the rest of the code samples, create an app.properties file in the sample-app folder and copy the following content:

```
licenseKey=XYFDLE
encrypt=false
```

Listing 8-3 shows the portion of sample-app's build.gradle file that assigns the two artifacts from this use case to archives configuration. You begin by declaring a reference to the app.properties artifact. Then you create a sourceJar task that would generate a JAR file with the source code and resource files in the src/main folder. Finally, you use the artifacts block to add the properties artifact and source JAR task to the archives configuration.

Listing 8-3. Associating artifact to configuration

```
def propertiesArtifact = file('app.properties')

task sourceJar (type : Jar) {
   classifier = 'sources'
   from sourceSets.main.allSource
}

artifacts {
   archives propertiesArtifact
   archives sourceJar
}
```

With this listing added to sample-app's build.gradle file, you can run the uploadArchives task and it will automatically deploy the two new artifacts along with the sample-app.jar file to the Maven repository. Running the command should yield this output:

```
\chapter8\sample-app>gradle uploadArchives
:compileJava UP-TO-DATE
:processResources UP-TO-DATE
:classes UP-TO-DATE
:jar UP-TO-DATE
:sourceJar
:uploadArchives

BUILD SUCCESSFUL
```

Upon successful execution of the command, navigate to the URL http://localhost:8081/nexus/content/repositories/snapshots/com/apress/gradle/intro/sample-app/1.0-SNAPSHOT/ in a browser. You should see the three artifacts shown in Figure 8-4.

sample-app-1.0-20151121.015904-5.jar

sample-app-1.0-20151121.015904-5.jar.md5

sample-app-1.0-20151121.015904-5.jar.sha1

sample-app-1.0-20151121.015904-5.pom

sample-app-1.0-20151121.015904-5.pom.md5

sample-app-1.0-20151121.015904-5.pom.sha1

sample-app-1.0-20151121.015904-5.properties

sample-app-1.0-20151121.015904-5.properties.md5

sample-app-1.0-20151121.015904-5.properties.sha1

sample-app-1.0-20151121.021255-6-sources.jar

Figure 8-4. *Sample app's three artifacts in Maven repo*

Open the `sample-app-1.0-###########.properties` file; it should contain the content shown in Figure 8-5.

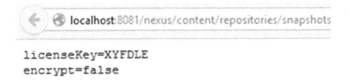

```
licenseKey=XYFDLE
encrypt=false
```

Figure 8-5. *Property file contents*

Installing to a Gradle Cache

In Chapter 6, you learned that Gradle maintains a cache where it stores downloaded artifacts and metadata. This improves build performance since the number of download requests made to external repositories is significantly reduced. By default this cache is located in the <<USER_HOME>>/.gradle/caches folder. Figure 8-6 shows a portion of Gradle cache located on our machine. Gradle computes a SHA1 hashcode of the artifact contents and uses it as the folder name for housing the artifact. Gradle doesn't guarantee this folder structure and it is quite possible that the structure may change with new Gradle versions.

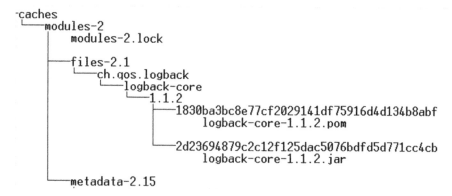

Figure 8-6. *Gradle cache directory structure*

Consider a scenario where you want to a third-party JAR file to be added to Gradle's cache so that it is available for Gradle builds. There could also be a different scenario where you have a project (called A) producing a JAR file that you want to be available in the Gradle cache for other projects to use. Folks with a Maven background quickly recollect the "install/install-file" goals provided by Maven (https://maven.apache.org/guides/mini/guide-3rd-party-jars-local.html) that allow you to add files to the Maven local cache. Gradle, on the other hand, treats its cache as a true cache and doesn't provide any mechanism to directly add JAR files.

To address these scenarios with Gradle, three options are discussed in the next subsections.

Use a File Repository

Add the third-party JAR files to a directory on your file systems. You can configure projects such as Project A in this scenario to publish generated artifacts to this directory. Projects needing to use the JAR files can use this directory as a file repository.

Use a Local Maven Repository

Publish JAR files to your local Maven repository and configure Gradle to pull dependencies from the Maven cache. Gradle projects using Maven can publish their artifacts to the local Maven repository using the `gradle install` command. For example, running `gradle install` in `sample-app` would make the `sample-app.jar` file available in local Maven repository, as shown in Figure 8-7.

Name	Type	Size	Dat
.m2 ▸ repository ▸ com ▸ apress ▸ gradle ▸ intro ▸ sample-app ▸ 1.0-SNAPSHOT			

Burn   New folder

Name ^	Type	Size	Dat
maven-metadata-local.xml	XML File	1 KB	12/
maven-metadata-remote.xml	XML File	1 KB	12/
maven-metadata-remote.xml.sha1	SHA1 File	1 KB	12/
resolver-status.properties	PROPERTIES File	1 KB	12/
sample-app-1.0-SNAPSHOT.jar	Executable Jar File	1 KB	11/
sample-app-1.0-SNAPSHOT.pom	POM File	1 KB	12/
sample-app-1.0-SNAPSHOT.properties	PROPERTIES File	1 KB	11/
sample-app-1.0-SNAPSHOT-sources.jar	Executable Jar File	1 KB	11/

Figure 8-7. *Sample app JAR in the local Maven repository*

Use a Central Repository

Publish the third-party JARs to a central repository such as Nexus. For JARs produced by projects such as project A, have a CI server build the project on a regular basis and push it to central repository. If the contents of these JAR files were to change often, the projects using the JAR file need to declare the dependency as changing. Here is an example of such a declaration:

```
dependencies {
    compile group:"com.apress", name:"A",version:"1.0-SNAPSHOT",changing:
true
}
```

Gradle by default caches artifacts marked changing for 24 hours. You can force Gradle to check for updated versions with every build by configuring its resolution strategy. Here is an example of such a configuration:

```
configurations.all {
    resolutionStrategy.cacheChangingModulesFor 0, "seconds"
}
```

Summary

In this chapter you reviewed Gradle's support for publishing artifacts. You learned that archives configuration is used to declare the artifacts produced by a project. You used `uploadArchives` to publish to a local file repository. Then you looked at installing Nexus Maven repository manager and used `mavenDeployer` to publish to a remote Maven repository. You also learned the configuration needed to deal with additional artifacts.

In the next chapter, you will review the concepts of continuous integration and explore a popular CI server, called Jenkins, and its support for Gradle.

■ ■ ■

CHAPTER 9

Continuous Integration

Continuous integration or CI is a software engineering practice where changes to source code are integrated into a shared mainline several times a day. Each change results in an automatic build that compiles and tests the entire code base. Any failures are immediately reported back, resulting in early detection of integration problems. Continuous integration also allows you to automatically monitor code quality, generate code coverage metrics, and assess overall project health.

The continuous integration market is filled with several open source and commercial tools such as Hudson, TeamCity, Bamboo, and Jenkins. This chapter explores Jenkins and its support for Gradle.

Continuous Integration Flow

Continuous integration servers interact with version control systems (VCS), such as SVN and GIT, to perform builds on a regular basis. A high-level interaction between CI and code repository is shown in Figure 9-1.

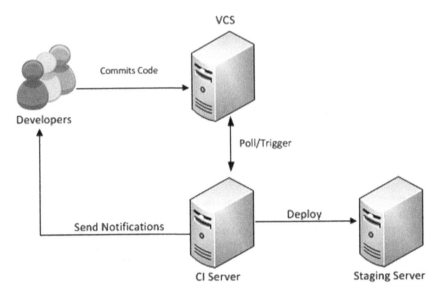

Figure 9-1. *CI flow*

The interaction begins with a developer checking in her changes to a central source code repository (VCS). The CI server can be configured to periodically poll for changes to the code repository or have the VCS trigger a build. When the CI server detects changes to code, it downloads the source code and begins a build. Upon a successful build, the CI server can push the generated artifacts to testing/staging environments. If any failures in the build are detected, the CI server sends out notifications to the developers.

Sample Project

To fully understand Jenkins support for Gradle, you need a sample Gradle project residing in a VCS. In this book, you will use Git as the VCS and GitHub, a popular online hosting service, for the Git repositories. You will be working with a sample application named ig-app that has been uploaded to GitHub at https://github.com/bava/ig-app. The sample project contains a simple build.gradle file and a HelloWorld.java class that prints "Hello World" to console.

To follow along with the rest of the chapter, you need an account on GitHub. If you are a first time user, you can sign up for a free account on GitHub's home page at https://github.com. Once you have an account, you need to *fork* or make a copy of the ig-app repository under your own account. This allows you to configure Jenkins to interact with your forked repository using your credentials. This also allows you to commit changes to the repository and have Jenkin builds triggered automatically. You can fork the ig-app repository by clicking on the Fork button next to the repository name, as shown in Figure 9-2.

Figure 9-2. *Forking the ig-app repository*

Installing Jenkins

Jenkins is an open source, cross-platform continuous integration tool written entirely in Java. It supports a wide variety of technologies and languages such as Java, .Net, PHP, Ruby, and more. Before you start using Jenkins, you need to install and configure it.

■ **Note**   Since Jenkins needs to interact with the Git repository, you need to have Git installed on your machine. You can download OS-specific Git installers at `http://git-scm.com/downloads`.

   Begin the Jenkins installation by downloading the latest version at `https://jenkins-ci.org/` (see Figure 9-3). Jenkins comes in two flavors—native installers for major operating systems and an executable WAR file. To keep things simple, this book takes the WAR file approach.

Figure 9-3. *The Jenkins download page*

Download the jenkins.war file and save it on your file system. Using a command prompt, navigate to the downloaded directory and run the following command to start Jenkins:

```
java -jar jenkins.war
```

Upon successful execution of the command, you should see the statement "INFO: Jenkins is fully up and running" on the console indicating that Jenkins is up and running. By default, Jenkins runs on port 8080. Using a browser, navigate to http://localhost:8080 and you should see the Jenkins dashboard, as shown in Figure 9-4.

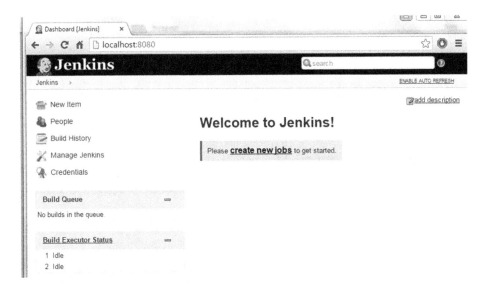

Figure 9-4. *The Jenkins dashboard*

Configuring Jenkins

Before you can start using Jenkins to run Gradle builds, you need to configure Jenkins by adding and configuring the Gradle and GitHub plugins. On the Jenkins dashboard's vertical navigation, click Manage Jenkins. Then click the Manage Plugins link. On the ensuing screen, click the Available tab and use the filter box to search for Gradle plugin, as shown in Figure 9-5.

Figure 9-5. *Available tab on the Manage Plugins screen*

Select the plugin and click the Download Now and Install After Restart button. Follow the same approach for searching and installing the GitHub plugin (see Figure 9-6).

Figure 9-6. *The GitHub plugin*

You will notice that the GitHub plugin will trigger the installation of other plugins, such as Git and Git Client (see Figure 9-7).

Installing Plugins/Upgrades

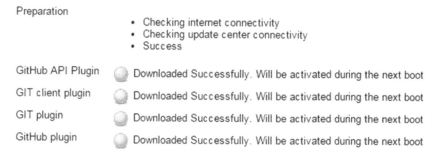

Figure 9-7. *Plugins installed with the GitHub plugin*

To complete the plugin installation, restart the Jenkins server. You can accomplish this by simply killing the Jenkins process at the command line (Ctrl+C on Windows) and rerunning the `java -jar jenkins.war` command.

Finally, you need to configure the Gradle plugin to use the local Gradle installation. To do this, click on the Manage Jenkins link on the dashboard and then click on the Configure System link. Navigate to the Gradle section on the page and click the Add Gradle button. This opens a section to configure Gradle installation. Enter **Local Gradle** as Gradle name. Then enter the Gradle installation directory under GRADLE_HOME and uncheck the Install Automatically option, as shown in Figure 9-8.

Gradle

Gradle installations   Gradle name
                                            Local Gradle

                                     GRADLE_HOME   C:\tools\gradle-2.7

                                         Install automatically

Figure 9-8. *The Gradle plugin configuration*

Save the changes by clicking the Save button at the bottom of the page. This concludes the plugin configuration and you can now move forward and create a Jenkins build job.

Creating the Build Job

Jobs in Jenkins represent tasks or steps in the build process. A build job for example can download source code and compile and execute tests. In this section, you will create a build job that executes the sample app's Gradle build script. To create a new job, follow these steps:

1. Navigate to the Jenkins dashboard at `http://localhost:8080` and click the New Item link. On the New Item screen, enter the name `intro-gradle-app` and select Freestyle Project, as shown in Figure 9-9. We chose the Freestyle Project option as it provides a lot of flexibility and can work with any SCM and build system. Click the OK button.

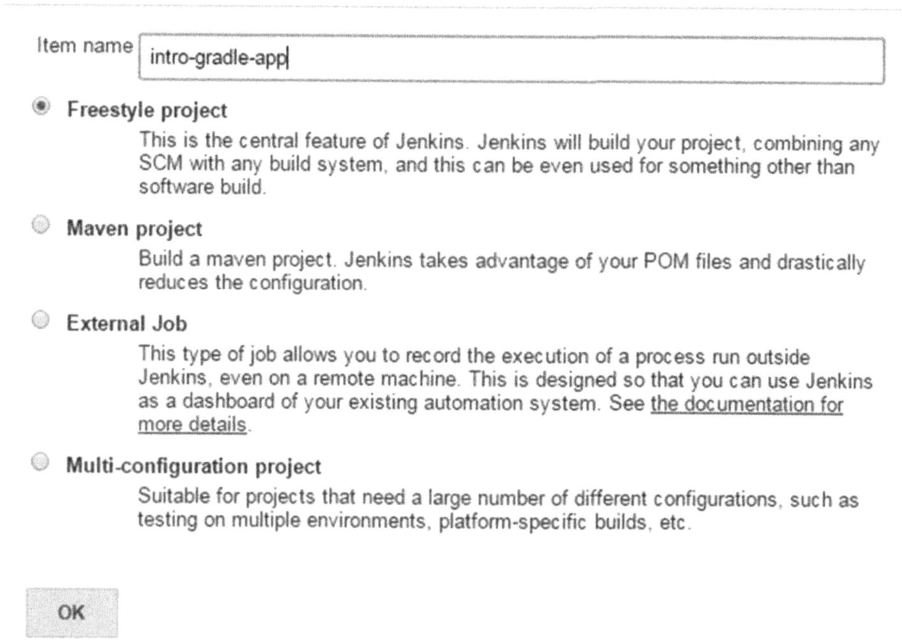

Item name | intro-gradle-app

◉ **Freestyle project**

This is the central feature of Jenkins. Jenkins will build your project, combining any SCM with any build system, and this can be even used for something other than software build.

○ **Maven project**

Build a maven project. Jenkins takes advantage of your POM files and drastically reduces the configuration.

○ **External Job**

This type of job allows you to record the execution of a process run outside Jenkins, even on a remote machine. This is designed so that you can use Jenkins as a dashboard of your existing automation system. See the documentation for more details.

○ **Multi-configuration project**

Suitable for projects that need a large number of different configurations, such as testing on multiple environments, platform-specific builds, etc.

OK

Figure 9-9. *New job screen*

2. On the next screen, enter the URL to your GitHub repository that contains the forked sample project (see Figure 9-10).

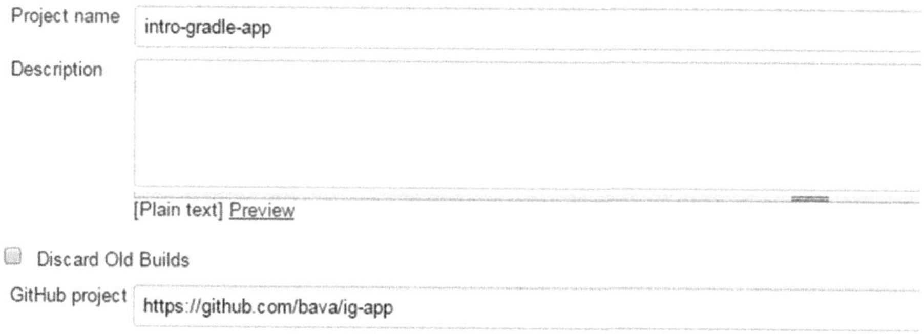

Project name | intro-gradle-app

Description |

[Plain text] Preview

☐ Discard Old Builds

GitHub project | https://github.com/bava/ig-app

Figure 9-10. *GitHub project URL*

3. Under the Source Code Management section, select the Git option. Under the Repository URL, enter the HTTPS URL to clone the GitHub repository, as shown in Figure 9-11.

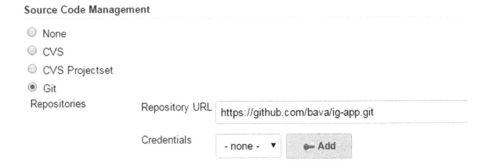

Figure 9-11. Source Repository configuration

4. You can obtain the clone URL to be entered on the GitHub repository page's vertical navigation (see Figure 9-12). Make sure that the HTTPS option is selected before copying the URL.

HTTPS clone URL

You can clone with HTTPS, SSH, or Subversion. ⦾

Figure 9-12. Clone URL to GitHub

5. Click the Add button next to the credentials. In the Add Credentials dialog box, enter your GitHub account's username and password, as shown in Figure 9-13. Click Add.

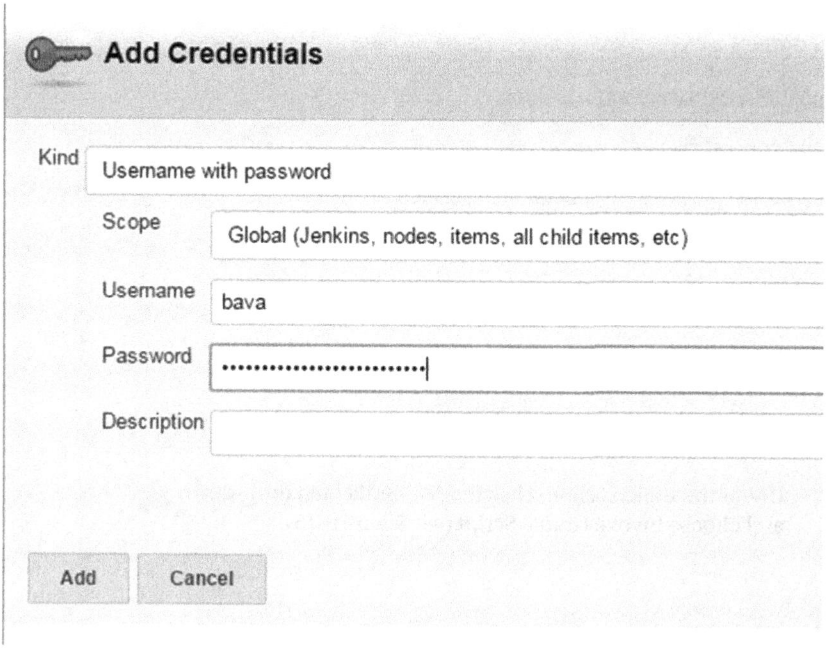

Add Credentials

Kind | Username with password

Scope | Global (Jenkins, nodes, items, all child items, etc)

Username | bava

Password | •••••••••••••••••••••••

Description |

Add   Cancel

Figure 9-13. *GitHub Repo credentials*

6. In the Build Triggers section, select the Poll SCM option. The schedule field takes a UNIX cron expression value. In Figure 9-14, H/15 * * * * has been entered, indicating that VCS should be polled every 15 minutes.

Build Triggers

☐ Build after other projects are built

☐ Build periodically

☐ Build when a change is pushed to GitHub

☑ Poll SCM

Schedule

H/15 * * * *

Figure 9-14. *The Build Triggers configuration*

7. Under the Build section, click the Add Build Step drop-down and choose Invoke Gradle Script (see Figure 9-15).

Build

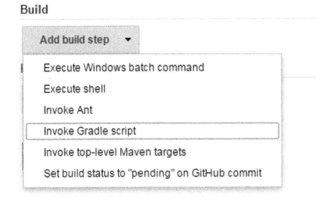

Figure 9-15. *Adding the build step*

8. Under the Invoke Gradle script section, select Invoke Gradle and, from the drop-down, select the Local Gradle option you configured in the preceding section (refer to Figure 9-8). Enter **clean build** in the Tasks textbox (see Figure 9-16).

▦ **Invoke Gradle script**

⦿ Invoke Gradle
Gradle Version

| Local Gradle |

◯ Use Gradle Wrapper
Build step description

Switches

Tasks

| clean build |

Root Build script

Build File

Specify Gradle build file to run. Also, some environment

Force GRADLE_USER_HOME to use workspace ▣

Figure 9-16. Invoke the Gradle script configuration

9. Click Save and you will be taken to the intro-gradle-app project page shown in Figure 9-17. From this page, you can trigger manual builds or change the job configuration.

Figure 9-17. *The intro-gradle-app project page*

Running the Build Job

The build job you configured in the previous section polls the repository for changes every 15 minutes. Additionally, you can use the project's page to trigger a manual build anytime. From Jenkins dashboard, click the intro-gradle-app project link (see Figure 9-18).

Figure 9-18. *Project list on dashboard*

On the ensuing project page, click the Build Now link on the left vertical navigation. This schedules a new build. Click on the build number and then click on Console Output, as shown in Figure 9-19.

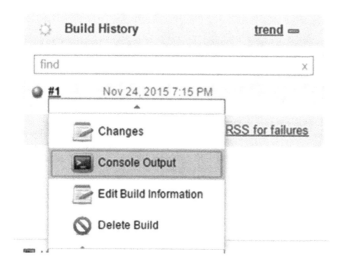

Figure 9-19. *Viewing the console output*

You should see the output of the execution, similar to Figure 9-20.

Console Output

```
Started by user anonymous
Building in workspace C:\Users\sbelida\.jenkins\jobs\intro-gradle-app\workspace
 > git.exe rev-parse --is-inside-work-tree # timeout=10
Fetching changes from the remote Git repository
 > git.exe config remote.origin.url https://github.com/bava/ig-app.git # timeout
Fetching upstream changes from https://github.com/bava/ig-app.git
 > git.exe --version # timeout=10
using .gitcredentials to set credentials
 > git.exe config --local credential.username bava # timeout=10
 > git.exe config --local credential.helper store --file=\"C:\Users\sbelida\AppD
timeout=10
 > git.exe -c core.askpass=true fetch --tags --progress https://github.com/bava/
 > git.exe config --local --remove-section credential # timeout=10
 > git.exe rev-parse "refs/remotes/origin/master^{commit}" # timeout=10
 > git.exe rev-parse "refs/remotes/origin/origin/master^{commit}" # timeout=10
Checking out Revision 6eab286b9f08ae83f9916d83cf111d2568781b2f (refs/remotes/ori
 > git.exe config core.sparsecheckout # timeout=10
 > git.exe checkout -f 6eab286b9f08ae83f9916d83cf111d2568781b2f
 > git.exe rev-list 6eab286b9f08ae83f9916d83cf111d2568781b2f # timeout=10
[Gradle] - Launching build.
[workspace] $ cmd.exe /C '"C:\tools\gradle-2.7\bin\gradle.bat clean build && exi
:clean
:compileJava
:processResources UP-TO-DATE
:classes
:jar
:assemble
:compileTestJava UP-TO-DATE
:processTestResources UP-TO-DATE
:testClasses UP-TO-DATE
:test UP-TO-DATE
:check UP-TO-DATE
:build

BUILD SUCCESSFUL
```

Figure 9-20. *Job execution output*

Archiving Artifacts

In the previous section, you ran a Jenkins build job to build the project and the generate ig-app.jar file. In this section, you will configure Jenkins to store those generated artifacts for later use.

From the Jenkins dashboard, navigate to the intro-gradle-app project page and click the Configure link on the left vertical navigation. Scroll to the bottom of the Configure page, click the Add post-build-action drop-down, and select the Archive the Artifacts option (see Figure 9-21).

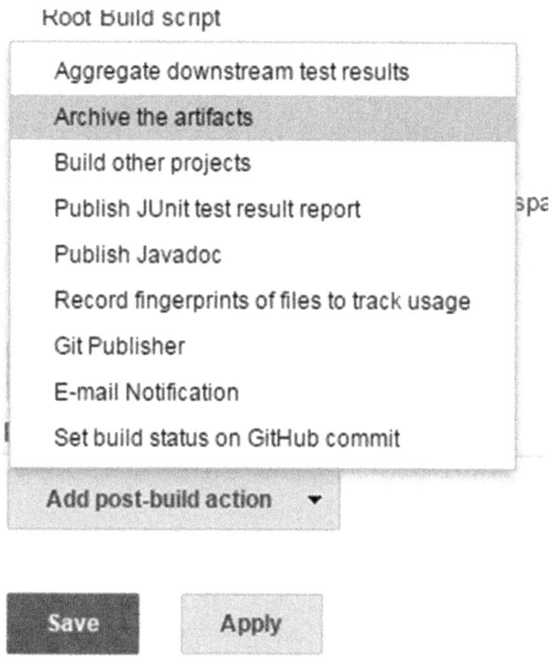

Root Build script

Aggregate downstream test results

Archive the artifacts

Build other projects

Publish JUnit test result report

Publish Javadoc

Record fingerprints of files to track usage

Git Publisher

E-mail Notification

Set build status on GitHub commit

Add post-build action ▼

Save   Apply

Figure 9-21. *Archive the artifacts post-build action*

In the Files to Archive textbox, enter the value build/**/*.jar to archive all generated JAR files (see Figure 9-22).

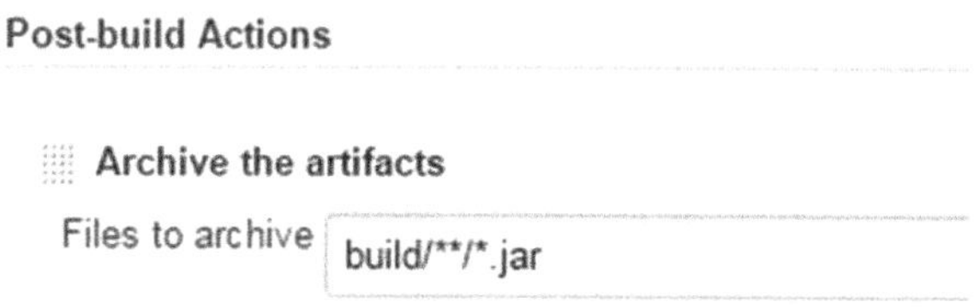

Post-build Actions

▒ **Archive the artifacts**

Files to archive | build/**/*.jar

Figure 9-22. *Files to archive configuration*

Save the configuration changes and trigger a manual build by clicking the Build Now button. Once the build is complete, the generated artifact should be available on the project dashboard, as shown in Figure 9-23.

Project intro-gradle-app

Workspace

Last Successful Artifacts
ig-app.jar   677 B view

Recent Changes

Permalinks

- Last build (#11), 26 sec ago
- Last stable build (#11), 26 sec ago
- Last successful build (#11), 26 sec ago
- Last failed build (#5), 11 days ago
- Last unsuccessful build (#5), 11 days ago
- Last completed build (#11), 26 sec ago

Figure 9-23. *ig-app.jar artifact on project dashboard*

Publishing Test Results

The Java plugin's test task runs unit tests and generates reports in HTML, XML, and binary formats. These reports display the number of tests run and helps you drill down to identify failed tests. By default the HTML reports are stored in the build/reports folder, while the XML/binary results are stored in the build/test-results folder.

The ig-app contains a JUnit test named HelloWorldTest in src/test/java. This unit test tests the functionality of the simple HelloWorld Java code. In this section, you will configure Jenkins to surface the generated reports on the project home page.

JUnit results in Jenkins are published through a post-build action. Navigate to the intro-gradle-app's configure page and select Publish JUnit Test Result Report (see Figure 9-24).

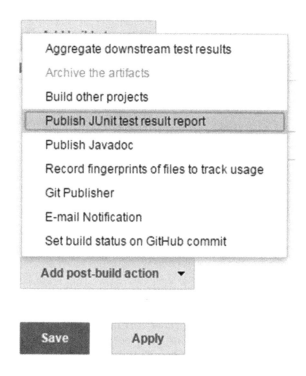

Figure 9-24. *Test result post-build action*

Enter the value build/test-results/*.xml in the Test Report XMLs textbox (Figure 9-25) and click Save button to save your changes.

Publish JUnit test result report

Test report XMLs

    build/test-results/*.xml|

    Fileset 'includes' setting that specifies the
    ☐ Retain long standard output/e

Health report amplification factor

    1.0

    1% failing tests scores as 99% h

Figure 9-25. *XML test report location config*

Trigger a new build. Upon successful completion, you should see the Latest Test Results link on the projects home page, as shown in Figure 9-26. Click the link and you should see test run details.

Latest Test Result (no failures)

Permalinks

- Last build (#12), 35 sec ago
- Last stable build (#12), 35 sec ago
- Last successful build (#12), 35 sec ago
- Last failed build (#5), 11 days ago
- Last unsuccessful build (#5), 11 days ago
- Last completed build (#12), 35 sec ago

Figure 9-26. *Test results on the project home page*

Summary

In this chapter, you learned about continuous integration flow and explored Jenkins, which is a popular open source CI server. You looked at installing Jenkins and configuring the necessary plugins to run your sample project located on a GitHub repository.

This discussion brings you to the end of the journey. Throughout the book, you have learned the key concepts behind Gradle. We hope you will use your newly found Gradle knowledge to automate and improve your existing build and project management processes.

Index

Get the eBook for only $5!

Why limit yourself?

Now you can take the weightless companion with you wherever you go and access your content on your PC, phone, tablet, or reader.

Since you've purchased this print book, we're happy to offer you the eBook in all 3 formats for just $5.

Convenient and fully searchable, the PDF version enables you to easily find and copy code—or perform examples by quickly toggling between instructions and applications. The MOBI format is ideal for your Kindle, while the ePUB can be utilized on a variety of mobile devices.

To learn more, go to www.apress.com/companion or contact support@apress.com.

Printed in the United States
By Bookmasters